GENDER, CONSTITUTIONS, AND EQUALITY

This book addresses whether the "gendering" of constitutions promotes women's equality.

The authors use a mixed-methods approach to explore how constitutional gender rights affect political processes and strategies, legislative and judicial outcomes, and ultimately women's equality. They employ a cross-national study by constructing a unique database of gender provisions in over 100 countries at three points in time: 1995, 2005, and 2015. Four in-depth comparative case studies on Argentina, Chile, South Africa, and Botswana trace the complex relationship between constitutional law, strategies, and policy change in four policy areas: family law, gender-based violence, reproductive rights, and employment rights. They argue that where egalitarian constitutional provisions are present, women's rights advocates can use them as a tool to fight gender discrimination and pursue policy changes that address gender-based power disparities.

At a time when gender equality provisions are increasingly common in constitutional design, this book clarifies the mechanisms that link constitutional provisions to changes in process and outcomes while also systematically describing and analyzing the effect of gender provisions across countries and over time. *Gender, Constitutions, and Equality* will inform theoretical debates on gender and politics, law and social change, feminist institutionalism, and constitutional design and its effect on legislation and political strategies.

Priscilla A. Lambert is Associate Professor of Political Science at Western Michigan University. She received her Ph.D. from the University of California San Diego in 2004 and specializes in comparative politics, Japanese politics, welfare state politics, and women and politics. She has published articles on these topics in *Comparative Politics*, *Gender and Politics*, the *Journal of Japanese Studies*, *Social Politics*, *Politics, Groups and Identities*, and the *Journal of Politics in Latin America.*

Druscilla L. Scribner is Professor of Political Science at the University of Wisconsin Oshkosh. She received her Ph.D. from the University of California San Diego in 2004 and specializes in comparative politics, Latin American judicial politics, and women and politics. She has published articles on these topics in *Comparative Politics*, *Gender and Politics*, *Global Policy*, *Politics*, *Groups and Identities*, and the *Journal of Politics in Latin America.*

Gender and Comparative Politics

The comparative research conducted in the field of gender and politics today is more than ever resulting in innovative theory building, applying novel research designs and engaging with mainstream political science. Gender & Politics has moved from the margins of political science to the center. Given the highly critical and activist roots of the gender and politics scholarship, it quasi naturally embraces intersectionality. The Routledge *Gender and Comparative Politics* book series aims to reflect this rich, critical and broad scholarship covering the main political science sub-disciplines with, for instance, gender focused research on political economy, civil society, citizenship, political participation and representation, governance and policy making.

Gendered Electoral Financing
Money, Power and Representation in Comparative Perspective
Edited by Ragnhild L. Muriaas, Vibeke Wang and Rainbow Murray

Women, Men, and Elections
Policy Supply and Gendered Voting Behaviour in Western Democracies
Rosalind Shorrocks

Gender, Constitutions, and Equality
A Global Comparison
Priscilla A. Lambert and Druscilla L. Scribner

For more information about this series, please visit: www.routledge.com/Gender-and-Comparative-Politics/book-series/GCP

GENDER, CONSTITUTIONS, AND EQUALITY

A Global Comparison

Priscilla A. Lambert and Druscilla L. Scribner

Routledge
Taylor & Francis Group
NEW YORK AND LONDON

Designed cover image: Martin Barraud

First published 2023
by Routledge
605 Third Avenue, New York, NY 10158

and by Routledge
4 Park Square, Milton Park, Abingdon, Oxon, OX14 4RN

Routledge is an imprint of the Taylor & Francis Group, an informa business

ISBN: 978-1-032-30164-8 (hbk)
ISBN: 978-1-032-30161-7 (pbk)
ISBN: 978-1-003-30372-5 (ebk)

DOI: 10.4324/9781003303725

Typeset in Bembo
by Apex CoVantage, LLc

Dedicated to all the wonderful women and girls in our lives

CONTENTS

FIGURES

TABLES

PREFACE AND ACKNOWLEDGMENTS

This book began as a conversation about teaching women and politics and comparative constitutionalism on our home campuses in the mid-2000s. It morphed into an initial quantitative study and then a National Science Foundation grant and fieldwork on two continents. In the years we have been engaged in this study, the interest in gender equality in constitutions has grown, as have the literature and the availability of data. This longitudinal project is informed by these developments in the broader scholarship on gender equality.

This research would not have been possible without the support of the NSF, which funded our fieldwork and research (Collaborative Research, Grant No. SES-0920998—Scribner and No. SES-0920990—Lambert). Any opinions, findings, or conclusions made in this book are those of the authors and do not necessarily reflect the views of the National Science Foundation.

From beginning to end, we have benefited from countless conversations with scholars, colleagues, family members, and friends, insightful comments and suggestions from conference panel discussants, and critiques and encouragement from anonymous reviewers. There have been graduate and undergraduate research assistants in our home institutions and abroad, and numerous scholars at universities and friends abroad who helped us get interviews, access archives, and just navigate our way through the different countries.

Early on we benefited from conversations with Merike Blofeld, Zach Elkins, Lisa Hilbink, and Jennifer Piscopo. Many individuals were incredibly helpful in both preparing for and carrying out fieldwork in Chile and Argentina, from making interview connections and hiring research assistants to finding places to stay with a 1-year-old in tow. Special thanks to Lisa Baldez, Lily Bravo, Mariana Carbajal, Lidia Casas, Natalia Gherardi, Aixa Granara, Susan Franceschet, Agustina Haime, Camila de la Maza, Mario Pecheny, Lucila Planich, Sybil Rhodes,

Marcela Ríos Tobar, and Catalina Smulovitz. We especially appreciate in-country assistance and institutional affiliation at the Universidad de Torcuato di Tella in Argentina, the Universidad de Diego Portales, and Universidad de Chile.

Similarly, we deeply appreciate numerous individuals who helped make our fieldwork a success in Botswana and South Africa: Gretchen Bauer, Hannah Britton, Jim Butterfield, Sushi Datta Sandhu, Rachel Ellett, Yvette Geyer, Charles Gossett, Amanda Gouws, Alex Huneeus, Heinz Klug, Ronald Letswela, Sheila Meintjes, Dorothy Mpabanga, Janet Olwage, Amy Poteete, Khadiya Richards, Mike Sibiya, Dee Smythe, Aili Tripp, and Jeremy Youde. Temporary institutional affiliation at the University of Botswana, Wits University, and the University of Cape Town in South Africa aided our data collection efforts.

For many others "in country" who we have not mentioned here by names, such as the incredible librarian at the Library of Parliament in Cape Town, or the taxi driver in Botswana who delivered us to the house past the tree that used to be on the corner, we will just say that we are so grateful for their time and efforts to improve this research project and help us get the data and information that we sought.

Special appreciation to Zach Elkins for multiple conversations about the Constitute database. Tracy Slagter, UWO colleague and friend, traveled to Cape Town to help with archival research and has been supportive throughout this project. Likewise, Kevin Corder at WMU has helped with statistics multiple times over the years and for this publication. We are also grateful to Kirsten Widner and anonymous reviewers who carefully read and commented on chapter drafts.

Institutional sabbatical support from Western Michigan University and the University of Wisconsin Oshkosh made field work possible during 2011 and 2012. The NSF support funded meaningful research experiences for multiple undergraduate and graduate political science students over several years. At WMU, the research assistants include Naomi Bick, Katie Bolter, Anna Clements, Marisha Lecea, Michael Miller, and Patrick McDaniel. At UW Oshkosh, Angelee Hammond helped keep track of a great cohort of UWO undergraduate research assistants, including Courtney Bichler, Marcus Taylor, Amy Gearhart, Brenna Ranzen, Martin McGee, Hope Schuhart, Alex Phillips, Amber Horak, Marissa Theyes, and Ava Tryon.

This project would not have been possible without the support of our husbands, children, and childcare providers.

1

GENDERING CONSTITUTIONS

Priscilla A. Lambert and Druscilla L. Scribner

Introduction

Do constitutional rights for women promote equality? Since the 1990s, women have played a growing role in the constitution-making process. Noting that law historically has not been gender-neutral, women have fought for and won constitutional rights that explicitly include women and recognize gender differences. In the constitutions of new democracies, gender equality provisions have become nearly standard. Most countries now recognize gender equality in their constitutions or include an anti-discrimination provision that explicitly states that discrimination on the basis of sex and other categories is illegal (Lambert and Scribner 2009; Young 2016). When women have been able to influence the writing of constitutions, these constitutions have tended to include a wide range of rights and protections (Dobrowolsky and Hart 2003; Irving 2008, 2017; Williams 2009).

The Brazilian Constitution, for example, includes numerous rights and guarantees related to gender: prohibitions on sex discrimination in salary, duties, and hiring criteria; free daycare and preschool for children up to age 6; a family allowance; maternity and paternity leave; special protection in the labor market for women; unemployment insurance; and a minimum wage. Similarly, the Namibian Constitution prohibits sex discrimination in all forms and recognizes that women, in particular, have been subject to discrimination and "need to be encouraged and enabled to play a full, equal and effective role in the political, social, economic and cultural life of the nation" (Article 23, Section 3). It obligates the state to enact legislation to "ensure the equality of opportunity for women, to enable them to participate fully in all spheres of society" (Article 95, Section a). South Africa's Constitution includes these rights and also explicitly

DOI: 10.4324/9781003303725-1

recognizes the right to physical and psychological integrity, which includes "the right to be free from all forms of violence from either public or private sources" as well as women's rights to "a) make decisions concerning reproduction; b) to security in and control over their body" (Chapter 2, Articles 12, 27).

In the last several decades, a number of countries have undertaken substantive reforms of the ways gender equality and gender differences are treated in their constitutions. The incorporation of gender and women into constitutional law, both conceptually and as an essential class of individuals, raises fundamental questions about the role of law in structuring social and political power and promoting (or hindering) gender equality and social change. Is women's equality enhanced by constitutional provisions that recognize gender differences and provide mechanisms to address the disadvantages that flow from sex-based or gender-role differences? Has explicit recognition of women's equality translated into greater social, political, and economic equality? Does constitutional recognition and valuation of care work contribute to greater gender equality? Do constitutional gender provisions challenge gendered power asymmetries, or do they recreate and perpetuate them?

We find that egalitarian provisions—provisions that promote women's substantive equality—are a powerful tool in the hands of women's rights advocates. Constitutional provisions, however, are neither self-enforcing nor self-interpreting; they do not constrain government power or bring about policy change on their own. Rather, constitutional provisions provide women's rights advocates with a legal anchor for legislative and judicial action, influence the content of legislation and judicial review of laws and policies, and help advocates fight gender discrimination and pursue policy changes that address gender-based power disparities. Where these constitutional provisions are weak or absent, women's rights advocates may have a limited capacity to pursue reforms. Likewise, where provisions tie women's citizenship to traditional gender roles, women's organizations may find that the constitutional discourse of maternalism limits them. They may face incentives to reduce the scope of demands for policy change or frame proposals in terms of women's maternal role rather than women's rights and equality. Moreover, groups and organizations who oppose women's rights also use the constitution; these groups draw upon these maternal provisions, on provisions that protect cultural rights, or exploit the absence of clearly defined constitutional rights to block progressive change.

Scholarship on the effects of constitutional change is part of the larger feminist institutionalism literature concerned with how institutions create, recreate, or challenge gendered power asymmetries (Krook and Mackay 2011; Chappell and Waylen 2013). Much of this literature focuses on the effects of gender quotas (Krook 2009; Freidenvall and Krook 2011; Franceschet and Piscopo 2008, 2013), women's policy agencies (Gouws 2004; Outshoorn and Kantola 2007; Squires 2007; and McBride and Mazur 2010), and federalism (Franceschet 2011; Vickers 2011; and Smulovitz 2015).

Although constitutions are powerful institutions that increasingly address gender, the feminist institutionalism scholarship to date tells us little about whether and how constitutional gender provisions increase women's equality in practice. Gender and constitutions research has been limited to constitutional design (Sullivan 2002; Irving 2008), to one or two case studies (Dobrowolsky 2000; Peters 1999; Ritter 2006), and to excellent but disparate theoretical and empirical contributions, many in edited collections (Williams 2009; Baines and Rubio-Marin 2005; Dobrowolsky and Hart 2003; Baines, Barak-Erez, and Kahana 2012; Young 2016; Irving 2017).

To understand whether constitutional gender provisions increase gender equality—and if they do, what the mechanism is—it is important to look systematically for patterns across the world. Until now, few studies have examined gender provisions comparatively or in a theoretically systematic way. Global studies include Austen and Mavisakalyan's (2016) examination of the relationship between non-discrimination clauses and women's representation in legislatures; Cassola, Raub, Foley, and Heymann's (2014) cataloging of gender provisions cross-nationally; and Irving's (2008) cross-national comparison of gender and constitutional design. The question that remains unanswered, however, is whether constitutional gender provisions as a whole materially affect women's rights advocacy or outcomes.

This book examines the relationship between constitutional gender provisions and gender equality. By doing so, we extend the literature on gender and law and feminist institutionalism in several ways. First, we focus on a neglected area of institutional analysis in comparative politics: constitutional law. Second, we create a typology of gender provisions and use a mixed methods research design to systematically describe and analyze the effect of gender provisions in national constitutions over time. This research design, which reflects multiple theoretical approaches to gender equality and gender difference, allows us to evaluate whether and how constitutional provisions that recognize gender difference and provide mechanisms to redress sex or gender-based disadvantages translate into greater social, political, or economic equality. Third, we explore both theoretically and empirically the role of constitutional gender provisions in promoting or hindering policy change and equality outcomes.

Why Constitutional Gender Provisions Matter

We begin with the premise that constitutions matter. While constitutions reflect the distribution of political power at the time of enactment, they also construct and shape social power. Constitutions provide a framework for government, mechanisms for the regulation and limitation of state authority, and protection of individual rights. In both democracies and non-democracies, constitutions have ideological components that constitute the political community and entrench shared ideals and values (Brown 2002; Okoth-Ogendo 1993). Constitutions and judicial review can "have a transformative effect on political discourse and the way fundamental moral and political controversies are articulated, framed, and settled" (Hirschl 2004, 13). Moreover, unlike legislation, constitutional provisions are difficult to alter.

While some scholars have argued that the law is unlikely to have an independent effect on social change (Strauss 2001; Hirschl 2004), others recognize the potential of law to influence social policy and rights and thus to contribute to progressive social change (Epp 1998; McCann 1994; Scheingold 2004). These scholars emphasize that social and political forces mediate the law's potential. The international law literature also emphasizes the role of rights advocates and transnational advocacy networks in the effectiveness of human rights treaties. In this view, constitutional provisions concerning gender equality, sex discrimination, and gendered social rights matter for women, but such provisions are not themselves a panacea (Baines and RubioMarin 2005; Banda 2005). Rights must be taken up by organized women's groups or they will remain nothing more than "parchment barriers."

Taken together, these scholarly works suggest several reasons constitutional provisions may be a powerful tool in the hands of women's rights advocates. Constitutional provisions inform constitutional interpretation, public policy, advocacy, and public discourse by helping define the possible and the aspirational. Constitutional rights, principles, and language legitimate (and occasionally challenge) relationships of power, whether social, economic, or political. The presence or absence of gender rights and provisions provides a clear indicator of state commitment to gender-related issues and sets the bar for judging whether government policy-making is consistent with these goals.

More specifically, constitutional gender provisions increase the legitimacy of rights claims, enable gender policy reforms, and provide legal tools and arguments in the courts. Gender provisions provide "an important enabling framework . . . contributing to substantial legal changes in women's civil and political rights" (Waylen 2007, 538). They can become a "rallying point" to overturn and oppose discriminatory legislation (Cassola et al. 2014) and be part of mutually reinforcing strategies of litigation, lobbying, and social mobilization (Duffy 2018). They prevent the erosion of hard-won rights when the political environment becomes more hostile to women's rights and equality. Clearly articulated constitutional rights and duties can also enhance the legitimacy of rights claims by women (Jagwanth and Murray 2005; O'Sullivan and Murray 2005). Women's rights provisions help establish a solid legal foundation for such claims and "provide women with tools to challenge state activity in the courts" (Baines and RubioMarin 2005, 9). Baldez, Epstein, and Martin (2006), for example, find that equal rights provisions increase the standard of the law that is applied and increase the likelihood of a favorable judicial decision for those asserting women's rights. The presence of constitutional rights may give courts greater leeway to interpret rights more broadly than legislated rights. In contrast, the absence of enumerated rights "puts pressure on the courts . . . to stretch their powers of statutory interpretation to its limits" (Fombad 2004, 143).

Gendering Constitutions: A Typology

Around the world, countries have chosen to recognize or ignore sex and gender in their national constitutions in ways that reflect differing conceptions or legal frameworks for equality. The terms *sex* and *gender* are often conflated. Women are marginalized and discriminated against because of their biological difference *and* because of their gender role in society. Gender-inclusive constitutional language and provisions across countries reflect both sex differences and gender roles. Newer constitutions tend to include both terms and additionally recognize sexual orientations as distinct categories. Older constitutions often just use the term *sex* or simply recognize that men and women are equal. We use these terms interchangeably. Throughout this book, we are concerned with how law can be used to tackle discrimination against women and improve equality.

Constitutional gender provisions recognizing sex and/or gender equality tend to reflect either a formal equality framework or a substantive equality framework. Formal equality constitutional provisions strive to be gender-neutral—they tend to recognize equality before the law for all citizens or for "men and women"—and may include a statement prohibiting sex discrimination. Formal equality provisions thus seek to remove formal barriers to equal treatment. For example, most U.S. Supreme Court decisions that have struck down sex-based classifications as discriminatory have been grounded in a formal equality framework. The Slovenian Constitution is a good example of a *formal equality approach*. Slovenia guarantees equality before the law with the following anti-discrimination statement: "In Slovenia, everyone shall be guaranteed equal human rights and fundamental freedoms irrespective of national origin, race, sex, language, religion, political or other conviction, material standing, birth, education, social status or any other personal circumstance" (Article 14, No. 1). The Constitution does not, however, contain other measures intended to level the economic or political playing field for women. Similarly, Article 1 of the Chilean Constitution states that "all persons are born free and equal," and Article 19 states that "men and women are equal before the law."

However, "a completely gender-neutral approach, . . . in reality seeks to assimilate women into a world constructed around male interests and male ways of seeing things" (Sachs 1990, 5). Substantive equality is a wider conceptualization of equality that highlights how gender-based differences, stereotypes, and reproductive and family roles systematically disadvantage women, presenting obstacles to the realization of equal rights and opportunities. A substantive equality framework makes it possible to recognize gender-based differences, including biological differences; to seek to redress disadvantage based on differences; and to view special treatment (positive or affirmative) action as an appropriate measure to achieve equality of outcomes. In many countries, substantive constitutional equality provisions, including those that obligate the state to act, exist alongside formal equality provisions.

Empirically, we tend to see two types of provisions that recognize gender and sex differences. Egalitarian constitutional provisions emphasize equality or a leveling of the political or economic playing field for women and "enable women to break through the layers of disability inherited from the past" (Sachs 1990, 5). Egalitarian provisions are often proactive; they obligate the state to redress the differences that gender makes in the opportunities women face in their economic, social, and political lives. For example, Germany's Basic Law lays out the principle that the "state supports the effective realization of equality of women and men and works towards abolishing present disadvantages" (Chapter 1, Article 3). Greece's Constitution establishes that the "adoption of positive measures for promoting equality between men and women does not constitute discrimination on the basis of sex. The State shall attend to the elimination of inequalities actually existing, especially to the detriment of women" (Part 4, Section 3, Article 116, No. 2). Some egalitarian provisions also seek to ensure women's safety through constitutional prohibitions of violence against women and state obligations to prevent violence. Such provisions are found, for instance, in the South African Constitution.

Maternal constitutional provisions, for their part, emphasize women's various needs as mothers and caretakers. Provisions such as maternity leave value and support women's caregiving role by recognizing gender-based obstacles related to motherhood and facilitating opportunities to combine formal employment and care work. State support for caregiving, for example, may help women achieve greater equality in the workplace. Yet these provisions can also perpetuate conservative values by privileging traditional marriage, family, and motherhood through institutionalized social rights that bind women's citizenship to their role as mothers.

Mexico's Constitution, for example, stipulates that pregnant women "shall not perform any work that requires considerable effort and presents a danger to their health in relation to their pregnancy" and provides for a fully paid maternity leave and rest periods for mothers nursing their infants (Title 6, Article 123). The Brazilian Constitution includes a range of substantive rights and guarantees similarly focused on supporting women's caregiving roles, maternity leave, special protection in the labor market, and a family allowance. Ireland's Constitution expressly recognizes and protects women's traditional role in the family in Article 41 with the following statements:

41.2.1 The State recognizes that by her life within the home, woman gives to the State a support without which the common good cannot be achieved.

41.2.2 The State shall, therefore, endeavor to ensure that mothers shall not be obliged by economic necessity to engage in labor to the neglect of their duties in the home. The State pledges itself to guard with special care the institution of Marriage, on which the Family is founded, and to protect it against attack.

Meanwhile, the 1987 Philippine Constitution outlines labor protections for women on the basis of motherhood: "The State shall protect working women by providing safe and healthful working conditions, taking into account their maternal function, and such facilities and opportunities that will enhance their welfare and enable them to realize their full potential in service of the nation" (Article 8, Section 14).

Overall, constitutional provisions fall into four broad types with respect to gender: no provisions, *gender neutral*, corresponding to the formal equality framework discussed earlier; *egalitarian*, approximating the substantive equality approach that is concerned with removing or overcoming gender-based barriers to equality; and *maternal*, a type of provision that reveres and reinforces women's maternal and caregiving roles. Constitutional provisions have the potential to affect gender outcomes because they provide a legal basis and focal point for women's rights advocacy and significantly influence the gendered content of subsequent legislation as well as the judicial review of laws and policies. These laws and policies, in turn, have important consequences for women's legal status and, ultimately, for women's social, political, and economic equality. Where gender provisions are absent, as in the gender-neutral constitutions, or entrench traditional gender roles, as the maternal provisions do, women's rights advocates and women's movements (and the political and institutional machinery of which they are a part) may have a limited capacity to pursue policies that contribute to gender equality. In contrast, substantive rights that are more egalitarian can make it easier for advocates to hold the state accountable, ensure that measures are implemented, and prevent backsliding.

A Mixed Methods Approach

To sort out the effects of constitutional provisions, we must ground theoretical claims in rigorous empirical research. Thus far, quantitative and qualitative research has shown mixed results concerning the effect of constitutional provisions, but few studies have combined the two approaches to test theories of constitutional provisions. Moreover, few systematic studies of gender provisions and their effects have been published. This book fills these gaps. We explore how constitutional gender provisions affect political processes, strategies, and ultimately gender equality using a cross-national quantitative study spanning three decades as well as in-depth case studies in two different regions.

We use quantitative analysis to test whether gender provisions matter more broadly for outcomes across countries and over time. In order to do this, we created a database of gender provisions in over a hundred countries at three points in time (1995, 2005, and 2015). The cross-national database is uniquely focused on gender provisions and systematically codes for all provisions that may impact women's social, economic, and political status; it codes 24 types of constitutional provisions that mention gender, women, sex, family, marriage, pregnancy, health, and so on.[1] This cross-national statistical analysis allows us to test for the effect of constitutional provisions against competing explanations in the literature. Using this database and cross-national measures of gender equality, we find that nations with more egalitarian constitutional provisions are more likely to have legal frameworks that protect women's rights and tend to enjoy higher scores on measures of women's equality with men than those with constitutions that emphasize women's familial and caregiving roles or those that are largely neutral toward gender.

In this statistical analysis, we also examine whether constitutional provisions and women's mobilization matter for outcomes that measure equality. Recent research has contributed important statistical analyses of whether constitutional provisions matter for human rights and other types of rights (Chilton and Versteeg 2016; Keith 2002; Keith, Tate, and Poe 2009; Melton 2014). Some of this research suggests that some rights are more enforceable than others because organized groups have an interest in pressuring the state to enforce these rights (e.g., economic rights and religious rights). That is, not all rights are created equal. However, most of these analyses do not test for the presence or strength of organized groups. To capture the influence of organized groups, we include Htun and Weldon's (2018) measures of the strength and autonomy of feminist organizations in our analysis.

Whereas the quantitative analysis helps us test whether constitutional provisions matter for equality across a large number of countries while statistically controlling for other factors, it does not reveal how provisions are used on the ground. Thus, we use case studies to explore how rights advocates deploy constitutional rights in their work and reveal the impact of their strategies on legislative and judicial processes and outcomes. In our two case studies of Argentina and Chile in Latin America and South Africa and Botswana in southern Africa, we trace the complex relationship between constitutional law, strategies, and policy change. Using archival research and interviews with women's rights advocates in each country, we compare how gender is constitutionalized and how these provisions have aided or hindered the advocates' efforts to achieve policy change in three key areas: gender-based violence, reproductive health, and employment. In the South Africa and Botswana case studies, we add a fourth policy area that is critical to women's rights in most African countries: customary law.

We selected these country cases using a most similar systems design: the countries in each regional pair are neighbors that share substantial cultural, historical, and economic similarities but differ in the ways gender is recognized in the constitution. Argentina and South Africa's Constitutions are egalitarian; Botswana and Chile's Constitutions are mostly neutral regarding gender, with some important exceptions, as we detail in the following.

The Argentine Constitution was reformed in 1994 after the country transitioned to democracy. The Constitution has several provisions intended to advance gender equality, including a constitutional gender quota (Article 37), recognition of the power of Congress to "legislate and promote positive measures guaranteeing true equality of opportunities and treatment" (Article 75, No. 23), and recognition and incorporation of the UN Convention on the Elimination of All Forms of Discrimination Against Women (CEDAW) (Article 75, No. 22). Women's rights advocates in Argentina have called these provisions "transformational."

In contrast, the 1980 Chilean Constitution does little to promote gender equality. Article 1 originally stated that "all men are born free and equal, in dignity and rights" but was amended in 1999 to ensure that all persons are equal and that "men and women are equal before the law" (Article 19, No. 2). Otherwise, it says nothing about gender equality. The Constitution singles out the family as the fundamental unit of society and obligates the state to take steps to protect and strengthen the family. Women's rights groups and many other groups and organizations have fought long and hard to rewrite the 1980 Constitution—a holdover from Pinochet's military regime. In October 2020, Chileans went to the polls and overwhelmingly voted in favor of writing a new constitution. We return to these efforts to draft a new constitution in the concluding chapter.

The South African Constitution guarantees individual rights and a wide array of social and cultural rights and establishes a clear commitment to overcoming past injustices while recognizing diversity (Bauer and Taylor 2005, 249). The Constitution includes the right to human dignity, a principle of non-sexism, and a strong and substantive equality clause. It specifies numerous rights for women, such as the right to freedom and security of the person and bodily autonomy, freedom from violence, reproductive choice, and a prohibition against any expression that amounts to advocating gender hatred. The Constitution requires courts to interpret legislation in the spirit of the Bill of Rights and to let international law and jurisprudence in other democracies guide judicial interpretation of the Bill of Rights. Like the constitutions of many African countries, the South African Constitution recognizes the right to celebrate traditional customs; however, it explicitly states that customary law must be consistent with the Bill of Rights. Customary law governs many areas of family law, including marriage and divorce, rights within marriage, division of shared property, inheritance, and child custody. In most cases, customary law does not grant women rights equal to those of their male relatives. Overall, the South African Constitution is one of the most progressive in the world, as measured by its effort to recognize women's differences, promote gender and racial equality, and redress past discrimination.

Botswana's Constitution was adopted in 1965 before the country held elections and gained independence in 1966. At the time, "women did not feature in political parties much at all" and enjoyed few political or economic rights

(Geisler 2004, 100). The Constitution mentions "sex" once when listing the fundamental rights and freedoms of the individual (Sections 3–15), and it uses "his and her" language in the descriptions of rights and freedoms. Section 15(3) initially prohibited discrimination against several categories, but not sex; however, the non-discrimination clause was amended in 2006 to include sex as one of the categories. Before the amendment, government officials maintained that sex discrimination did not violate the Constitution.[2] Botswana's Constitution, unlike South Africa's, specifically exempts customary law from the equality and nondiscrimination provisions.

We examined legislation, legislative debates, and high court decisions in each country between 1990 and 2020. In all four countries, we also interviewed women's rights advocates working within the state, in women's organizations, and in legal advocacy to remove discriminatory laws and judicial decisions and push for greater equality for women.

In Argentina and South Africa, legislation, policy debates, and high court decisions often reflect the constitutional commitment to gender equality and are likely to obligate the state to act to fulfill its constitutional guarantees. Gender provisions are a tool that advocates use in numerous ways: to set the agenda, to educate (legislators, judges, and the public) and raise awareness, to justify laws in parliamentary debates, to block discriminatory laws, to determine which cases to pursue in a litigation strategy, to weigh in on litigation through the submission of amicus briefs, and to strengthen their cases in court with rights-based reasoning. Egalitarian provisions may even help bring about cultural shifts in discourse. In Chile, legislation and legislative debates reflect competing frames of reference, one stressing gender-neutral equality and the other stressing family protection. Gender-specific bills emphasizing women's role within the family (rather than gender equality) have a better chance of passing. Similarly, customary law provisions hinder rights claims in Botswana. In both countries, rights advocates believe their constitutions do not enhance the legitimacy or feasibility of their efforts. Moreover, the absence of explicit gender rights often forces advocates to use second-best strategies—usually appeals to international laws and treaties—to pursue their goals.

Organization of the Book

Do gender provisions matter for women's equality? We answer this question through a quantitative analysis of about 150 countries between 1995 and 2015 and case studies of two country pairs with constitutions that differ significantly concerning gender provisions.

Chapter 2 develops the theoretical framework, introduces our gender provisions database, and lays out the methods by which we test our hypotheses. We draw upon scholarship addressing law and social change, research on gender and politics, and the international law and advocacy literature to identify the ways constitutional rights and protections can impact policy and court decisions. This research suggests that constitutions are important because they provide an enabling framework and enhance the legitimacy of rights-based arguments in legislatures and the courts. We emphasize that while constitutions are a tool, their usefulness hinges on whether civil society, particularly women's rights advocates and organizations, takes up these rights.

Our empirical study begins in Chapter 3 with a quantitative analysis. We use our database of gender provisions in national constitutions in over 100 countries at three time periods (1995, 2005, and 2015) to evaluate whether these provisions are associated with greater legal protection and women's equality. We look at gender provisions and their relationship to laws and legal frameworks in four policy areas: violence against women, reproductive rights, labor equality, and customary law. We then assess the effects of egalitarian and maternal provisions on women's equality in a panel data analysis. This statistical analysis allows us to test for the effect of gender provisions while controlling for alternative explanations.

Chapter 4 is a case study of Chile and Argentina. The chapter compares advocacy, legislation, and litigation strategies and outcomes in Argentina and Chile between 1990 and 2020. Although Chile and Argentina share many social, political, and historical characteristics, they differ regarding gender rights in their national constitutions in important ways. Drawing upon legislation, legislative debates, high court decisions, and interviews, we trace how advocates view the constitution and how it does or does not matter for their advocacy efforts. We then compare how the constitution is used to pursue women's rights policy in three policy areas: gender-based violence, employment, and sexual and reproductive rights.

In Chapter 5, we consider another pair of similarly situated countries with constitutions that differ significantly in their approach to gender: Botswana and South Africa. South Africa has one of the most progressive constitutions in the world and includes many gender rights and provisions on affirmative action. In contrast, Botswana's 1965 Constitution includes a sex equality statement but no other gender rights. This case study follows a structure similar to that of the Argentina–Chile chapter. However, in addition to considering policy and litigation outcomes for gender-based violence, employment, and sexual and reproductive rights, it examines customary law, which is critical to women's rights in most African countries.

In Chapter 6, we pull together the qualitative and quantitative evidence from the empirical chapters to answer the question: Do constitutional rights matter for women's equality? First, we look cross-regionally and consider our two countries with egalitarian constitutions (Argentina and South Africa) compared to those with gender-neutral constitutions (Botswana and Chile). This allows us to highlight similar strategies and outcomes, despite regional differences. We find that where constitutional provisions for gender equality are substantive, as in South Africa and Argentina, gender provisions are central to civil society actors' activities for policy change advocacy and legal mobilization. In Botswana and Chile, the absence of egalitarian provisions has encouraged advocates to reach around the national constitution and rely on international law to legitimate their claims and fight for favorable policies and court decisions. We then consider the quantitative and qualitative results in tandem. Finally, we briefly review recent efforts to review and reform the constitution in Botswana and Chile and the potential implications for women's equality.

Notes

1 Details on coding methods and the database are in Chapters 2 and 3.
2 The government argued that "the omission of sex in the non-discrimination clause was intentional and was made in order to permit legislation in Botswana which was discriminatory on grounds of sex" (Fombad 2004, 144).

References

Austen, Sioban and Astghk Mavisakalyan. 2016. "Constitutions and the Political Agency of Women: A Cross-country Study." *Feminist Economics* 22, no. 1: 183–210.

Baines, Beverley and Ruth Rubio-Marin. 2005. "Introduction: Towards a Feminist Constitutional Agenda." In *The Gender of Constitutional Jurisprudence*, edited by Beverly Baines and Ruth Rubio-Marin, 1–21. Cambridge: Cambridge University Press.

Baines, Beverley, Daphne Barak-Erez, and Tsvi Kahana, eds. 2012. *Feminist Constitutionalism: Global Perspectives*. Cambridge: Cambridge University Press.

Baldez, Lisa, Lee Epstein, and Andrew Martin. 2006. "Does the US Constitution Need an Equal Rights Amendment?" *Journal of Legal Studies* 35: 243–283.

Banda, Fareda. 2005. *Women, Law and Human Rights: An African Perspective*. Oxford and Portland. Oregon: Hart Publishing.

Bauer, Gretchen and Scott D. Taylor. 2005. *Politics in Southern Africa: State and Society in Transition*. Boulder: Lynne Reinner.

Brown, Nathan J. 2002. *Constitutions in a Nonconstitutional World Arab Basic Laws and the Prospects for Accountable Government*. New York: Suny Press.

Cassola, Adèle, Amy Raub, Danielle Foley, and Jody Heymann. 2014. "Where Do Women Stand? New Evidence on the Presence and Absence of Gender Equality in the World's Constitutions." *Politics & Gender* 10, no. 2: 200–235.

Chappell, Louise and Georgina Waylen. 2013. "Gender and the Hidden Life of Institutions." *Public Administration* 91, no. 3: 599–615.

Chilton, Adam S. and Mila Versteeg. 2016. "Do Constitutional Rights Make a Difference?" *American Journal of Political Science* 60, no. 3: 575–589.

Dobrowolsky, Alexandra. 2000. *The Politics of Pragmatism: Women, Representation, and Constitutionalism in Canada*. Oxford: Oxford University Press.

Dobrowolsky, Alexandra and Vivien Hart. 2003. "Introduction: Women, New Politics and Constitutional Change." In *Women Making Constitutions: New Politics and Comparative Perspectives*, edited by Alexandra Dobrowolsky and Vivien Hart, 1–19. New York: Palgrave Macmillan.

Duffy, Helen. 2018. *Strategic Human Rights Litigation: Understanding and Maximising Impact*. Oxford: Hart Publishing.

Epp, Charles. 1998. *The Rights Revolution: Lawyers, Activists, and Supreme Courts in Comparative Perspective*. Chicago: University of Chicago Press.

Fombad, Charles Manga. 2004. "The Constitutional Protection Against Discrimination in Botswana." *International and Comparative Law Quarterly* 53: 139–170.

Franceschet, Susan. 2011. "Gender Policy and State Architecture in Latin America." *Politics and Gender* 7, no. 2: 273–279.

Franceschet, Susan and Jennifer M. Piscopo. 2008. "Gender Quotas and Women's Substantive Representation: Lessons From Argentina." *Politics and Gender* 4, no. 3: 393–425.

Franceschet, Susan and Jennifer Piscopo. 2013. "Equality, Democracy, and the Broadening and Deepening of Gender Quotas." *Politics and Gender* 9, no. 3: 310–316.

Freidenvall, Lenita and Mona Lena Krook. 2011. "Discursive Strategies for Institutional Reform: Gender Quotas in Sweden and France." In *Gender, Politics, and Institutions: Towards a Feminist Institutionalism*, edited by Mona Lena Krook and Fiona Mackay, 42–57. New York: Palgrave Macmillan.

Geisler, Gisela. 2004. *Women and the Remaking of Politics in Southern Africa*. Uppsala: Nordiska Afrikainstitutet.

Gouws, Amanda. 2004. "The Politics of State Structures: Citizenship and the National Machinery for Women in South Africa." *Feminist Africa* 3: 1–12.

Hirschl, Ran. 2004. *Towards Juristocracy: The Origins and Consequences of the New Constitutionalism*. Cambridge: Harvard University Press.

Htun, Mala and S. Laurel Weldon. 2018. *The Logics of Gender Justice: State Action on Women's Rights Around the World*. New York: Cambridge University Press.

Irving, Helen. 2008. *Gender and the Constitution Equity and Agency in Comparative Constitutional Design*. New York: Cambridge University Press.

Irving, Helen (ed.). 2017 *Constitutions and Gender*. Cheltenham: Edward Elgar Publishing.

Jagwanth, Saras and Christina Murray. 2005. "No Nation Can Be Free When Half of It Is Enslaved." In *The Gender of Constitutional Jurisprudence*, edited by Beverly Baines and Ruth Rubio-Marin, 230–255. Cambridge: Cambridge University Press.

Keith, Linda Camp. 2002. "Constitutional Provisions for Individual Human Rights (1976–1996): Are They More Than Mere Window Dressing?" *Political Research Quarterly* 55: 111–143.

Keith, Linda Camp, C. Neal Tate, and Steven Poe. 2009. "Is the Law a Mere Parchment Barrier to Human Rights Abuse?" *The Journal of Politics* 71, no. 2: 644–660.

Krook, Mona Lena. 2009. *Quotas for Women in Politics: Gender and Candidate Selection Reform Worldwide*. New York: Oxford University Press.

Krook, Mona Lena and Fiona Mackay (eds.). 2011. *Gender, Politics, and Institutions: Towards a Feminist Institutionalism*. New York: Palgrave Macmillan.

Lambert, Priscilla A. and Druscilla L. Scribner. 2009. "A Politics of Difference vs. a Politics of Equality: Do Constitutions Matter?" *Comparative Politics* 41, no. 3: 337–357.

McBride, Dorothy E. and Amy G. Mazur. 2010. *The Politics of State Feminism: Innovation in Comparative Research*. Philadelphia: Temple University Press.

McCann, Michael. 1994. *Rights at Work: Pay Equity Reform and the Politics of Legal Mobilization*. Chicago: University of Chicago Press.

Melton, James. 2014. "Do Constitutional Rights Matter?" unpublished paper. Available at: https://pdfs.semanticscholar.org/e030/faaef3401760e608dfb9faa13389bd41d377.pdf.

Okoth-Ogendo, H. W. O. 1993. "Constitutions Without Constitutionalism: An African Political Paradox." In *Constitutionalism and Democracy: Transitions in the Contemporary*

World, edited by Douglas Greenberg, Stanley N. Katz, Steven C. Wheatley, and Melanie Beth Oliviero, 65–80. Oxford University Press.

O'Sullivan, Michelle and Christina Murray. 2005. "Brooms Sweeping Oceans? Women's Rights in South Africa's First Decade of Democracy." *Acta Juridica* 17: 1–41.

Outshoorn, Joyce and Johanna Kantola (eds). 2007. *Changing State Feminism*. Basingstoke, UK: Palgrave.

Peters, Anne. 1999. *Women, Quotas, and Constitutions: A Comparative Study of Affirmative Action for Women Under American, German, EC and International Law*. London: Kluwer Law International.

Ritter, Gretchen. 2006. *The Constitution as Social Design: Gender and Civic Membership in the American Constitutional Order*. Stanford: Stanford University Press.

Sachs, Albie. 1990. "Judges and Gender: The Constitutional Rights of Women in a Post-Apartheid South Africa." *Agenda: Empowering Women for Gender Equity* 6, no. 7: 1–11.

Scheingold, Stuart. 2004. *The Politics of Rights: Lawyers, Public Policy, and Political Change*, second edition. Ann Arbor: University of Michigan Press.

Smulovitz, Catalina. 2015. "Legal Inequality and Federalism: Domestic Violence Laws in the Argentine Provinces." *Latin American Politics and Society* 57, no. 3: 1–26.

Squires, Judith. 2007. "The Challenge of Diversity: The Evolution of Women's Policy Agencies in Britain." *Politics and Gender* 3, no. 4: 513–530.

Strauss, David. 2001. "The Irrelevance of Constitutional Amendments." *Harvard Law Review* 90: 1457–1505.

Sullivan, Kathleen M. 2002. "Constitutionalizing Women's Equality." *California Law Review* 90, no. 3: 735–764.

Vickers, Jill. 2011. "Gendering Federalism: Institutions of Decentralization and Power-Sharing." In *Gender, Politics, and Institutions*, edited by Mona Lena Krook and Fiona Mackay, 129–146. Basingstoke: Palgrave Macmillan.

Waylen, Georgina. 2007. "Women's Mobilization and Gender Outcomes in Transitions to Democracy: The Case of South Africa." *Comparative Political Studies* 40, no. 5: 521–546.

Williams, Susan. 2009. "Introduction: Comparative Constitutional Law, Gender Equality, and Constitutional Design." In *Constituting Equality: Gender Equality and Comparative Constitutional Law*, edited by Susan Williams, 1–28. Cambridge: Cambridge University Press.

Young, Katharine G. 2016. "Introduction: A Public Law of Gender?" In *The Public Law of Gender: From the Local to the Global*, edited by Kim Rubenstein and Katharine G. Young, 1–40. Cambridge: Cambridge University Press. DOI:10.1017/CBO9781316481493.003.

2

WHY CONSTITUTIONS MATTER FOR GENDER EQUALITY

Priscilla A. Lambert and Druscilla L. Scribner

Introduction

Almost 50 years ago, Ruth Bader Ginsberg made the case for the Equal Rights amendment on the basis of legislative and judicial effects:

> Yes, the job of revising outmoded sex-based laws could be done without an ERA. But history strongly suggests the task will remain on the legislative backburner absent the stimulus explicit constitutional commitment would supply. . . . Just as the ERA should end legislative inertia that keeps outdated laws on the books, so the amendment should relieve judicial anxiety, the uneasiness judges feel in the gray zone between interpretation and alteration of the Constitution.
>
> *(Ginsberg 1979, 174–175)*

Today, women's rights advocates are still seeking women's rights in the constitution. Constitutions structure political power; they also structure and construct social power. This is particularly the case in the context of gender (Dobrowolsky and Hart 2003; Irving 2008; Williams 2009). Constitutional rights, principles, and language legitimate and value (and sometimes challenge) relationships of power, whether social, economic, or political. Constitutions provide enforceable rules for regulating and limiting state power and protecting individual rights, and unlike legislation, these provisions are difficult to alter. Constitutional language, principles, and specific provisions inform constitutional interpretation, public policy, advocacy, and public discourse by helping to define the possible and the aspirational. They provide women's rights advocates with a constitutional anchor for legislative and judicial action and influence the content of legislation and

DOI: 10.4324/9781003303725-2

judicial review of laws and policies (Scribner and Lambert 2010; Lambert and Scribner 2020).

Much of our understanding of constitutional provisions comes from the law and social change and the international law literature. This scholarship can be roughly divided into two groups: qualitative studies that focus mostly on how constitutional provisions or human rights treaties affect the policy process and rights advocates' strategies and quantitative studies that test whether constitutional rights and provisions (or human rights treaties) are associated with better outcomes, as measured by higher scores on human rights outcomes, environmental policy, or enforcement of civil and political rights in general.

This chapter draws on the law and social change and the international law and domestic politics literature to clarify how constitutional provisions matter for these processes and lays out our research design, which uses quantitative and qualitative methods to determine whether gender provisions are associated with more women-friendly outcomes. Throughout the book, we consider the effect of constitutional provisions on *process* and *outcomes*. The qualitative case studies examine both process and outcomes, and the statistical analysis tests the effect on outcomes only. By *process*, we mean the way advocates use constitutional rights to challenge the status quo or defend legislative gains. By *outcomes*, we mean legislative reforms and high court decisions that block or remove discriminatory laws, legislation that enhances gender equality, and ultimately women's standing compared to men.

We contend that constitutional gender provisions affect both process and outcomes because egalitarian provisions can enhance the legitimacy of policy proposals, contribute to an enabling framework, and provide advocates with the legal tools to challenge state and private action in the courts. Consequently, the ways gender equality and difference are recognized shape the strategies with which women's rights advocates and their opponents pursue policy changes. The forms this recognition takes also affect the content of subsequent legislation, the judicial interpretation of laws and constitutional rights, and even women's equality in practice.

Why Constitutions Matter for Gender Policy and Gender Equality

Whether women's equality can be furthered by constitutional recognition is closely related to a fundamental debate about the effect of the law on society and social change. One perspective is that the law is not transformative and does not independently affect social change (Rosenberg 1996; Hirschl 2004; Strauss 2001). Rather, the law reflects the ideology or interests of the dominant classes or groups when the law or constitution was written. For example, Strauss (2001) argues that constitutional amendments are "irrelevant" and serve only to "ratify changes that have already taken place in society" (1459). Likewise, in his comparative analysis of constitutional development in four countries, Hirschl (2004) contends that the effect of constitutions on distributive justice is often "overrated if not outright negligible" and "appears to have only a limited capacity to advance progressive notions of social justice" (13). That is, other factors influence social outcomes regardless of whether particular laws or constitutional provisions are in place.

The alternative perspective asserts that the law and courts can be important mechanisms for advancing progressive social causes but that the effects are mediated by social and political actors (Epp 1998; McCann 1994; Scheingold 2004). While Scheingold (1974, 2004) was skeptical of reform-oriented legal mobilization and recognized the conservative nature of law and courts, he also viewed law and rights as resources that disadvantaged groups could mobilize. Similarly, McCann (1994) argued that a strong citizen's movement is critical to effective laws: "law . . . can be, in the hands of defiant citizens, a source of disorder and egalitarian reordering" (ix).

Feminist scholars agree that constitutional provisions concerning gender equality, sex discrimination, and gendered social rights matter for women when they are used as part of a broad strategy for legal and social change. However, constitutional provisions are not a panacea (Baines and RubioMarin 2005; Banda 2005), nor can a constitution "in itself secure rights for women" (Jagwanth and Murray 2005, 231; Jackson 2017). As Dobrowolsky and Hart (2003, 3) contend, "only constant vigilance and the hard grind of sustained activism ensure that over time textual promises are honoured and . . . women's lives change for the better." Thus, constitutional gender provisions help to secure policy and social change to the extent that rights advocates take them up.

Studies on the domestic impact of international law parallel the law and social change literature. There is considerable debate about whether international treaties matter at the domestic level. Those who argue that it does matter pay attention to the critical role of rights advocates in the domestic and international arenas (Grugel and Peruzzotti 2007; Hafner-Burton and Tsutsui 2005; Neumayer 2005). This literature on transnational advocacy networks suggests that international law, in the hands of rights advocates, can make it possible to disseminate information and raise awareness, increase the legitimacy of rights claims, use law to socialize a population and its leaders, set standards with which to hold leaders accountable, and facilitate mobilization (Grugel and Peruzzotti 2012; Keck and Sikkink 1998; Hafner-Burton, LeVeck and Victor 2016; Simmons 2009; Craske and Molyneux 2002). Similarly, the law and social change literature has found that the law may have broad non-policy effects related to social movements, including attracting media attention, changing actors' consciousness of what might be possible, changing judicial attitudes, and motivating other forms of advocacy, including protest (Albiston and Leachman 2015; McCammon and McGrath 2015).

Constitutions by themselves do not constrain government power and do not produce social or legal change. Constitutional provisions must be taken up, claimed, and used by political and social actors in service of such goals in the political context of their time. We contend that constitutional provisions provide women's rights advocates with a constitutional anchor for legislative and judicial action and influence the content of legislation and judicial review of laws and policies (Lambert and Scribner 2020). While we treat constitutional gender equality provisions as an institutional variable that shapes behavior, strategies, and outcomes, we also recognize that the provisions themselves are the product of social and political change (Przeworski 2004). Furthermore, "constitutional rights are never interpreted or implemented in a political or ideological vacuum" (Hirschl and Sachar 2005, 228).

In every country, there is a significant gap between women's rights on paper and in reality. Policy implementation and enforcement issues can and do undermine the overall effectiveness of constitutional and legal guarantees. These issues deserve close examination but are beyond the scope of this study. Our goal in this book is to explore the possible links between constitutional rights, mid-range legislative and judicial processes, and broader outcomes measuring equality without ignoring the social and political conditions in which actors are embedded. The way gender equality is constitutionalized enhances the legal legitimacy of equality-based arguments and provides women's rights advocates with the legal tools to pursue various objectives, including legislation and litigation. In the following section, we examine these claims and lay out our theoretical expectations.

Theoretical Expectations

Enhances the Legitimacy of Rights Claims

Clearly articulated rights and duties can enhance the legitimacy of rights claims (Jagwanth and Murray 2005; O'Sullivan and Murray 2005). Constitutional provisions are a source of legitimacy because they are "reflections of shared values" (Ginsburg and Huq 2014, 121) and can shape "the kinds of legal claims that can be made as well as the persuasiveness of those claims" (Andersen 2009, 12). For example, O'Sullivan and Murray (2005) argue that "[t]he clear commitment to gender equality in the [South African] Constitution has transformed the framework within which women's rights are claimed and given the demands of women a legitimacy that they did not have before" (40).[1] This framework matters because "legal framing is often an effective way of packaging a movement's demands because the pervasiveness and cultural legitimacy of law make legal language resonate with a wide cross-section of audiences" (Albiston and Leachman 2015, 547). Similarly, the international law literature notes that framing an issue as a human rights issue can lend legitimacy to social movements, making rights claims more compelling. Such framing is an integral part of efforts to socialize political leaders and the public (Hafner-Burton et al. 2016; Goodman and Jinks 2013; Tsutsui, Whitlinger, and Lim 2012).

We expect that constitutional commitments to gender equality will provide political and legal legitimacy for gender policy and ground arguments for gender policy change, whether this change is being sought through legislative, administrative, or judicial action. Evidence of this relationship should be observed in terms of the *process* of policy advocacy and reform in the qualitative case studies. Thus, we expect a discourse of constitutionally recognized gender rights to be reflected in the language used to introduce, frame, and debate gender policy. Women's rights arguments and proposals should be less politically controversial in countries with egalitarian gender provisions, where constitutional values about gender equality are explicit and thus provide more constitutional legitimacy for such arguments than in countries with neutral or maternal provisions. For example, advocates will likely refer to the constitution and constitutional rights to justify women-friendly laws in parliamentary debates more often than advocates in countries that do not have these constitutional guarantees.

In contrast, we expect to see greater reliance on international law in countries with constitutions that do not have egalitarian provisions, as these constitutions do not provide a robust legal platform for gender equality. That is, international law may serve as an alternate source of legal legitimacy for reform efforts.

Enables Policy Change

Scholars contend that constitutional provisions can be part of an enabling framework that provides "scaffolding" for political and legal change (Waylen 2007, 538; Albertyn 2019, 775). There are numerous ways constitutional provisions might enable advocates in their work and facilitate social change. The international law literature is beneficial here, as scholars have laid out different paths by which international law can influence domestic political processes and outcomes.

Studies on law and social change and international law and transnational advocacy have found that the law may have broad *process* effects. These include attracting media attention and raising awareness, disseminating information, educating the public and political leaders, and even changing attitudes (Hafner-Burton et al. 2016; Keck and Sikkink 1998; McCammon and McGrath 2015; Neumayer 2005). When leaders make arguments or propose laws that violate constitutional rights, advocates can use the constitution to hold them accountable. Beyond the broad legitimacy effects of international law, scholars have argued that the ratification of human rights treaties "helps advocates detect, punish, and deter by setting standards and providing the means to discipline violators" (Hafner-Burton et al. 2016, 167).

Constitutional rights may also enable policy reform by facilitating mobilization. Both constitutional law and international law scholars have argued that the presence of legal rights can "empower advocates and mobilize stakeholders" and encourage underrepresented groups to mobilize for social change (Hafner-Burton and Tsutsui 2005; McCann 1994; Scheingold 2004; Simmons 2009).

Constitutional rights may even expand actors' consciousness of what is possible, changing attitudes and motivating other forms of advocacy, including protest (Albiston and Leachman 2015; McCammon and McGrath 2015). For example, McCann's (1994) study of the Equal Pay Act finds that pay equity litigation attracted media attention, helped mobilize activists, and attracted new participants to the movement (McCann 1994, 140–153).

Women's movements can use egalitarian constitutional provisions as a tool to fight gender discrimination and pursue policy changes that address gender-based power disparities. Constitutional rights and guarantees set standards and can be particularly useful to those seeking to repeal discriminatory laws and prevent the passage of new laws that are discriminatory. In egalitarian constitutions, gender provisions provide a foundation for rights claims. Thus, we would expect policymakers and women's rights advocates in these countries to identify these provisions as a central tool with which to pursue policy change.

The output of the policy process—legislation and policy reform—is also informed, facilitated, or thwarted by constitutional provisions. In France, for example, the incorporation of substantive equality statements was followed by "a flurry of legislative activity . . . to promote gender equality" (Suk 2017, 421). In countries with gender egalitarian rights and provisions, we expect to see different policy *outcomes*, such as legislation that promotes equal rights, in terms of both content and the number of laws; legislation that draws on egalitarian language in the constitution; and the use of egalitarian provisions to challenge and block discriminatory laws. In countries with few or no egalitarian provisions, we expect their absence to be a constraint on advocates seeking policy change and to limit their ability to remove or prevent discriminatory legislation and policy.

If egalitarian provisions matter for legislation and litigation outcomes, then they should lead to better outcomes for women more generally. Thus, in the quantitative analysis, we expect such rights to be associated with higher scores on measures of women's equality with men in the political, economic, and social arenas. In the case studies where egalitarian constitutional provisions are weak or absent, women's movements and the political and institutional machinery of which they are a part may have a limited capacity to pursue gender policy reform and rely more heavily on international laws and treaties.

However, not all rights are the same. Some types of provisions may be part of an enabling framework, while others may counter or negate the potential impact of equal rights provisions, bolstering more traditional gender values in the constitution. In particular, where constitutional language ties women's citizenship to traditional gender roles, ignores gender differences, or emphasizes the rights and protections of the family, women's rights advocates and policymakers may find themselves constrained by a constitutional discourse of gender neutrality or maternalism. They may also face incentives to reduce the scope of their demands for policy change or frame proposals in terms of women's maternal role rather than women's rights and equality. When rights activists must frame the debate in terms of women's traditional caregiving role to gain conservative support, their efforts often produce, at best, a watered-down version of reforms that do little to advance women's rights (Blofield and Haas 2005). Some protections, such as Bulgaria's constitutional protection of women in the workforce, are so paternalistic that they correspond to a loss of welfare (Lucas 2009). Thus, maternal provisions and provisions centered on the state's obligation to protect the family may undermine reform efforts.

In addition, some constitutional provisions may counter or nullify rights guarantees in other parts of the constitution. This is the case with exemptions for cultural rights and customary law,[2] which may actively undermine equal rights and non-discrimination provisions. For example, Botswana's Constitution guarantees fundamental rights for men and women but simultaneously states that customary laws are exempt (Chapter 2, Section 15, No. 4); customary law trumps constitutional rights to equality and non-discrimination (Fombad 2004). South Africa's Constitution also recognizes cultural rights and customary law but specifically prohibits any custom that contradicts the rights enumerated in the Constitution.

Provides Legal Tools and Arguments That Facilitate Litigation

Constitutional rights affect the judicial interpretation of laws and the protection and advancement of those rights in the courts. They can "create or limit opportunities for NGOs to frame their legal claims persuasively" (Vanhala 2017, 384). Where constitutional rights for women's equality are enumerated, the resulting legal foundation for rights claims can "provide women with tools to challenge state activity in the courts" (Baines and Rubio-Marin 2005, 9). The way gender equality is recognized affects legal processes and outcomes.

In terms of *process*, the presence or absence of egalitarian provisions can influence the decision to pursue a litigation strategy and the choice of cases to take. The legal opportunity literature focuses on the rules and institutions that affect a social movement's willingness to take claims to the courts, such as access to the courts, the cost of litigation, and judicial receptivity (De Fazio 2012; Epp 1998). Gender provisions that include a "constitutional enforcement mechanism" that empowers individuals or public interest groups to bring a case to court create opportunities for litigation seeking to protect or advance rights (Lucas 2009; UN Women 2017, 71).[3] The presence of specific constitutional rights may encourage advocates to take cases they think they can win, perhaps with the result of overturning discriminatory laws and practices. Alternatively, advocates may take on cases they will likely lose to raise awareness of discriminatory treatment that conflicts with constitutional rights.

For advocates to pursue litigation, the judiciary has to have "some receptiveness to the legal claims" asserted. The nature of courts, including judicial culture, is a key feature of the legal opportunity structure (Andersen 2009; Hilson 2002; Vanhala 2017). The presence of egalitarian provisions can influence the judicial culture, and combined with training and more women in the courts, can help increase receptiveness to women's rights claims. Overall, we expect that egalitarian provisions will facilitate litigation based on gender rights claims and influence judicial awareness of gender rights.

With regard to *outcomes*, gender rights and provisions may contribute to more favorable judicial decisions. In their comparative study of the effect of US state-level equal rights amendments (ERA), Baldez, Epstein, and Martin (2006) found that the presence of an ERA provision in state constitutions increased "the likelihood of a court applying a higher standard of law . . . [and] the likelihood of a decision favoring the equality claim" in the adjudication of sex discrimination cases (Baldez et al. 2006, 246). The presence of constitutional values and enumerated rights gives judges a constitutional anchor. As Scheingold (1974) noted, "judges are unlikely to take the lead on behalf of goals that are not firmly rooted in constitutional values." While the absence of enumerated rights: "puts pressure on the courts . . . to stretch their powers of statutory interpretation to its limits" (Fombad 2004, 143). Egalitarian provisions have also been used to litigate discriminatory laws and practices, including customary and religious traditions that subordinate women to men.[4]

If gender provisions in the national constitution improve the opportunity to advance litigation on women's rights and increase the chances of women-friendly decisions, we expect to see more judicial decisions favoring women's rights claims in our country cases with egalitarian constitutions than in countries with neutral or maternal constitutions.

Comparing Constitutions and Gender Equality

To test whether gender provisions matter for process and outcomes, we use a mixed methods approach that includes in-depth case studies and large-n quantitative analysis. The quantitative study in Chapter 3 uses our coding of constitutions to test whether gender provisions are associated with outcomes such as more gender equality (as measured by cross-national gender gap scores). The case studies in Latin America and southern Africa allow us to look at processes and outcomes that are more closely linked to constitutional provisions in four countries and examine how gender provisions shape advocacy, strategy, and, ultimately, outcomes in the legislative and judicial arenas.

A Database of Constitutional Gender Provisions

To examine differences in gender provisions in national constitutions over time, we created an original database of gender provisions in national constitutions between 1995 and 2015. For consistency of translation, we relied almost entirely on two sources for national constitutions: Constitutions of the Countries of the World (subscription service)[5] and the Constitution Project's Constitute Database.[6]

Each constitution was double-coded and then reconciled to produce a single cross-national database of gender provisions over 20 years. The UN Women's Global Gender Equality Constitutional Database served as an additional reference when reconciling coding differences.[7] A few countries, such as the United Kingdom, do not have written constitutions. In these cases, we included documents with constitutional status (e.g., The United Kingdom's Human Rights Act of 1998 and The Equality Act of 2006).

Each national constitution was coded for 24 types of rights and guarantees related to women, sex, gender, family, and motherhood. The database draws on and extends our previous cross-national study (Lambert and Scribner 2009) and offers a way to differentiate between the constitutions that guarantee citizens' rights to gender equality and those that make it the state's responsibility to ensure gender equality. The 24 topics cover equal rights, anti-discrimination, and the status of international law. They also include guarantees, rights, and protections for the family, pregnant women, and affirmative action in the political, social, and economic arenas (see Appendix A for a complete list).

This database is unique in several regards: it provides a comprehensive review of gender provisions in national constitutions from equality and non-discrimination statements to reproductive rights and rights to bodily integrity; it systematically codes these provisions and assigns a numerical score so that the presence or absence of these provisions can be used to test hypotheses about the impact of gender provisions quantitatively; it allows us to use these scores to create a typology of constitutions, and it scores the relative strength of the different rights and guarantees.

Each constitution is coded at three points in time—1995, 2005, and 2015—for the presence or absence of a particular gender provision. The constitutions are scored progressively such that provisions that obligate the state to act to remove barriers to gender equality receive higher scores. For example, in the area of sex discrimination, the coding method distinguishes between the presence of a simple non-discrimination statement on the basis of sex, the constitutionality of positive measures to overcome past discrimination, and the obligation of the state to pursue those kinds of measures and level the playing field for women. Mongolia and Ethiopia offer such a contrast. Mongolia's Constitution states that "No person shall be discriminated against on the basis of ethnic origin, language, race, age, sex, social origin and status, property, occupation and position, religion, opinion, and education. Everyone shall be a person before the law" (Article 14, No. 2). This statement receives a point for recognition of sex-based discrimination. Ethiopia's Constitution, in contrast, goes considerably further. Article 35, the Rights of Women, recognizes the following:

35.3 The historical legacy of inequality and discrimination suffered by women in Ethiopia taken into account, women, in order to remedy this legacy, are entitled to affirmative measures. The purpose of such measures shall be to provide special attention to women so as to enable them to compete and participate on the basis of equality with men in political, social, and economic life as well as in public and private institutions.

35.4 The State shall enforce the right of women to eliminate the influences of harmful customs. Laws, customs, and practices that oppress or cause bodily or mental harm to women are prohibited.

Because of Ethiopia's recognition of the state's obligation to overcome past discrimination and the constitutionality of positive discrimination, the Constitution receives a high score for non-discrimination.[8] Countries with no provision prohibiting discrimination based on sex, such as the U.S. Constitution, receive a score of 0.

Gender Provisions Across Countries and Across Time

Tables 2.1, 2.2, 2.3, and 2.4 present a summary of gender provisions across countries in 1995, 2005, and 2015. In Table 2.1, we present the percentage of countries that included a gender-specific equality statement ("men and women are equal") and a gender-specific non-discrimination statement. We also show whether affirmative action is constitutional and the status of international law in the legal hierarchy of the country. As these tables make clear, gender-specific constitutional provisions have become more common over time. The biggest change is the notable increase in equal rights and non-discrimination statements. For example, whereas gender equality statements were present in 47% of constitutions coded in 1995, by 2015, 60% of constitutions specifically stated that all are equal regardless of sex or that men and women are equal. Non-discrimination statements that recognize sex as a category were already present in 58% of constitutions in 1995, and this percentage increased to 72% by 2015. A significant proportion of constitutions not only say that sex discrimination is unconstitutional but also specify that affirmative action policies to redress gender discrimination (or other types of discrimination) are constitutional; some go further by obligating the state to pursue such policies. It has become standard to include one or both of these provisions; in 2015, only 13% of our 164 constitutions had neither an equality statement nor a non-discrimination statement.[9]

TABLE 2.1 Constitutional gender equality rights, 1995–2015

	1995 *N = 100*	*2005* *N = 136*	*2015* *N = 164*
Equal rights statement	47%	54%	60%
Non-discrimination statement	58%	64%	72%
• Positive discrimination is constitutional	20%	19%	24%
International law has constitutional status	21%	24%	31%

TABLE 2.2 Constitutional political rights, 1995–2015

	1995 *N = 100*	*2005* *N = 136*	*2015* *N = 164*
Political participation	19%	27%	36%
• **Principle of equality**	14%	18%	22%
• **State obligation or multiple statements about equal participation**	5%	9%	14%
Equal suffrage	9%	16%	18%
Equal citizenship	13%	20%	28%
Gender quota	6%	9%	17%

Table 2.2 summarizes the constitutional provisions related to women's political participation. Gender-specific suffrage statements have increased over time—many include a gender-neutral statement guaranteeing universal adult suffrage. In 1995, 15% of constitutions included a statement about equal participation for women being a guiding principle, and another 5% obligated the state to take action to ensure women's equal participation in the political arena. By 2015, those percentages had increased to 22% and 14%, respectively. Similarly, the presence of constitutional gender quotas for representative or other governing bodies increased from 7% to 17% in this period. Many constitutions specify that no more than two-thirds of the legislature members may be of one gender; others do not specify a minimum. For example, Article 27, Section 8 of the Kenyan Constitution specifies that "the State shall take legislative and other measures to implement the principle that not more than two-thirds of the members of elective or appointive bodies shall be of the same gender." India and Belgium have similar provisions. Argentina's constitutional gender quota guarantees equality of opportunity but leaves specific rules to parties and the electoral system. In contrast, Tunisia's Constitution is left vague: "The state seeks to guarantee women's representation in elected bodies" (Article 34).

Table 2.3 summarizes how social rights have changed (or stayed the same) over the 20-year period. The percentage of constitutions with marriage equality statements, neutral and gender-specific combined, has hovered around 35%. Similarly, the number of constitutions that include special social security provisions for mothers or pregnant women has seen little change. However, there has been a gradual increase in the percentage of constitutions with family protection provisions, reproductive rights, and gender-based violence provisions. In 1995, only 3% of constitutions included a gender-specific statement or right related to violence against women. In 2015, 13% of constitutions included a gender-specific right to freedom from violence and/or the state's obligation to protect women from violence.

For example, Bolivia's Constitution was revised twice in this period, with each revision adding stronger statements on gender-based violence. In 2002, the

TABLE 2.3 Constitutional social rights, 1995–2015

	1995 N = *100*	*2005* N = *136*	*2015* N = *164*
Marriage equality	33%	35%	35%
• **Spousal equality**	13%	15%	16%
• **Gender-specific**	20%	20%	19%
Reproductive rights	10%	11%	14%
• **Child spacing**	5%	6%	8%
• **Right to reproductive services**	5%	5%	6%
Gender-based violence	4%	7%	13%
• **Gender-specific statement**	1%	4%	5%
• **State obligation to protect**	3%	3%	8%
Family protection	57%	61%	66%
• **Important social unit**	7%	8%	10%
• **Right to protection**	33%	38%	43%
• **State obligation and/or multiple statements**	17%	15%	13%
Anti-abortion	10%	10%	11%
• **Life begins at conception**	10%	10%	10%
• **Explicit ban on abortion**	0%	0%	1%

Constitution was revised to include sexual and family violence: "Any kind of torture, coercion, extortion, intimidation, or other form of physical, moral or sexual violence is hereby prohibited. Any kind of violence within the family is also prohibited" (Article 12). In 2009, a more explicit statement of women's rights (warranting our highest score on gender-based violence) was added in Article 15:

15.1 Every person has the right to life and physical, psychological, and sexual integrity. No one shall be tortured, nor suffer cruel, inhuman, degrading, or humiliating treatment. The death penalty does not exist.

15.2 Everyone, in particular women, has the right not to suffer physical, sexual, or psychological violence, in the family as well as in the society.

15.3 The State shall adopt the necessary measures to prevent, eliminate, and punish sexual and generational violence, as well as any action or omission intended to be degrading to the human condition, to cause death, pain, and physical, sexual, or psychological suffering, whether in public or private spheres.

Similarly, Thailand strengthened its constitutional provision from a statement about the right of children and family members to state protection from violence (Constitution of Thailand 1997, Section 53) to an explicit statement that includes women: "Children, youth, women and family members shall have the right to be protected by [the] State against violence and unfair treatment and shall have the right to medical treatment or rehabilitation upon the occurrence thereof"

TABLE 2.4 Constitutional economic rights, 1995–2015

	1995 *N = 100*	*2005* *N = 136*	*2015* *N = 164*
Equal pay/equal work	33%	32%	33%
• **Gender-neutral**	12%	10%	11%
• **Gender-specific**	21%	22%	22%
Equal opportunity in the workplace	35%	35%	39%
• **Gender-neutral**	17%	17%	17%
• **Gender-specific**	15%	14%	16%
• **State obligation and/or multiple statements**	3%	4%	6%
Family leave	5%	5%	6%
Maternity leave	18%	17%	16%
Labor protection based on gender or pregnancy	31%	33%	31%
• **Gender-specific**	21%	24%	22%
• **State obligation and/or multiple statements**	10%	9%	9%

(Constitution of Thailand 2007, Section 52). The 2007 Constitution also provides for protection in the judicial process in cases of sexual offenses (Section 40).

Finally, Table 2.4 summarizes constitutional economic rights, such as equal pay for equal work and provisions for maternity leave. These rights have not changed greatly over time. Gender-neutral and gender-specific statements about the right to equal pay for equal work are found in about 33% of constitutions over the 20-year period. Provisions for equal opportunity for women in the workplace have slightly increased.

Building a Typology of Gender in Constitutions

Not all gender provisions are the same. Egalitarian provisions emphasize women's equality, while others emphasize women's reproductive role or their role within the family. To assess constitutional gender provisions, we cannot simply add up the number of gender rights and protections in a country's constitution. Rather, we need to consider whether these different types of provisions undermine or reinforce each other. The coding method allows us to differentiate among gender-specific constitutional provisions that are *egalitarian, maternal*, and *neutral*. Egalitarian provisions recognize biological and gender-based differences and seek to redress disadvantages based on gender, often through positive or affirmative actions, as noted earlier. These provisions relate to gender-inclusive equality statements, non-discrimination provisions, equal political participation directives, gender quotas, the status of customary law, marriage equality, reproductive health rights, gender-based violence, equal pay for equal work, workplace equality, and family leave. Figure 2.1 shows how countries differ with respect to egalitarian provisions (Chapter 3 details how the provision scores are calculated).

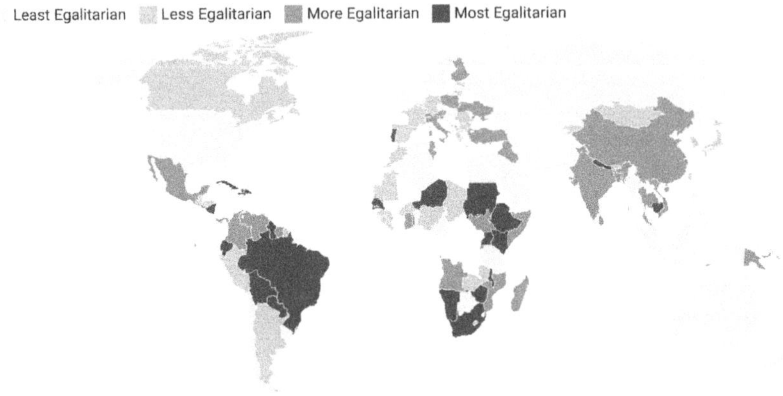

FIGURE 2.1 Range of egalitarian constitutional provisions in 164 countries, 2015

Constitutional provisions that emphasize women's different needs as mothers and caretakers we term *maternal*. These gender provisions include those concerned with family protection, maternity leave, workplace protection, and social rights directed at women as mothers specifically. Some provisions categorize women with other vulnerable groups, such as children, the elderly, and the mentally or physically disabled. These are similarly coded progressively, such that provisions that obligate the state to act (a state duty, for example) receive higher scores. High scores in these areas indicate a strong constitutional commitment to protecting and supporting women's maternal and familial roles. Figure 2.2 depicts countries according to the number and strength of maternal provisions. Maternal provisions may improve women's social or economic condition, but they can also reinforce traditional roles and limit women's ability to achieve full equality. The right to state protection of the family can also exercise such an effect.[10] Such provisions may prove to be a hindrance to women's rights because the family can be a source of social control, "a site of relative power and subordination for women" (Hunter 2006, 63).

Low scores or a zero on most coding questions indicate a *gender-neutral* approach in the constitution. That is, some constitutions provide for health care, education, and/or social and economic rights but include no gender-specific statements. For example, Article 28 of the Estonian Constitution includes a gender-neutral right to social assistance: "Estonian citizens shall be entitled to state assistance in the case of old age, inability to work, loss of a provider, and need." Similarly, Indonesia's Constitution guarantees that "Every person shall have the right to social security in order to develop oneself fully as a dignified human being" (Article 28H, No. 3). Although Estonia's and Indonesia's social rights are included in the database, they do not count toward the egalitarian or maternal score.

National constitutions have different mixes of gender provisions. While some countries have all three types of provisions, most tend to include a cluster of

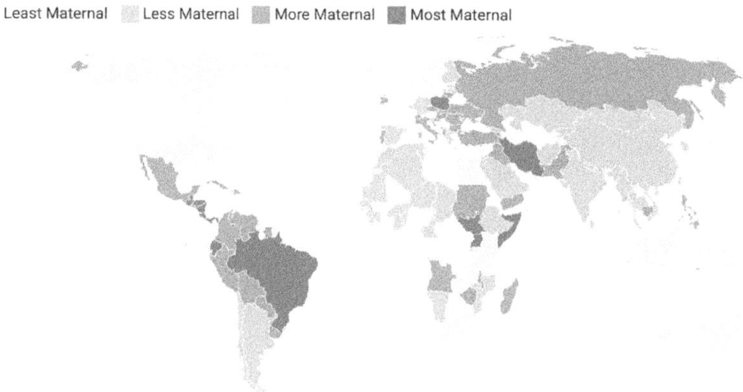

FIGURE 2.2 Range of maternal constitutional gender provisions in 164 countries, 2015

provisions of the same type. This tendency allows us to create a typology of constitutions: *egalitarian, maternal*, and *neutral*.

Figure 2.3 shows egalitarian and maternal provision scores for select countries. Countries in the lower right corner have egalitarian constitutions that include an equal rights statement and/or a strong non-discrimination statement as well as provisions that proactively promote gender equality (and few maternal provisions). Countries concentrated in the upper left-hand corner have maternal constitutions that feature provisions that support and protect women's traditional caregiving role, value women as mothers and wives, and reinforce gender role-based citizenship, perhaps with an equality statement or non-discrimination statement but with little else on women's rights. Those with few enumerated gender rights of any sort are in the bottom left corner and are categorized as neutral. Gender-neutral constitutions tend to recognize equality before the law for all citizens and may include a non-discrimination statement, recognizing sex as one among several categories of individuals.

Not all constitutions fit neatly into our constitution typology. Several constitutions include both egalitarian and maternal provisions. For example, Brazil, Mexico, and Ukraine have gendered rights to equality, strong non-discrimination provisions, and state obligations to promote women's equality in the political, economic, and social arenas while also protecting maternity rights and pregnancy in these same arenas. In our statistical analysis, we use constitutional provision scores for both types of gender rights.

It is important to note that the database codes not only for the presence of rights provisions but also for provisions that undermine gender rights. For example, if the constitution states that "men are born free and equal," as Chile's did until 1999, it is scored as a negative one in our equal rights category.[11] Similarly,

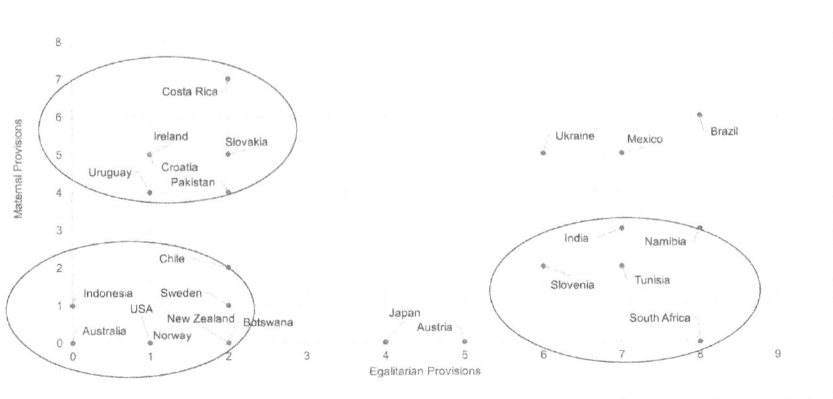

FIGURE 2.3 Gender provisions and constitutional typology

countries that only pass citizenship through the father (or husband) scored a negative one on citizenship equality.

One of the provisions most likely to undermine gender equality and women's status is customary law or personal law, which is often found in plural legal systems.[12] Customary law guarantees cultural rights that govern marriage, inheritance, divorce, and custody. Customary law is, without exception, discriminatory against women. As noted earlier, many constitutions enumerate equal rights for men and women and/or forbid discrimination based on sex but simultaneously have a clause that subsumes these rights under customary law—often labeled "cultural rights." In other words, customary law trumps individual rights when there is a conflict between the two. For example, the Constitution of Botswana not only guarantees equal rights for men and women but also exempts customary or personal law:

> 2.15 no law shall make any provision that is discriminatory . . . this section shall not apply to any law in so far as that law makes provision . . . c) with respect to adoption, marriage, divorce, burial, devolution of property on death or other matters of personal law.

Such clauses are not uncommon in African and South Asian constitutions. Other plural legal systems recognize customary law but subordinate it to constitutional law or civil law. South Africa's Constitution includes such a provision: "The [cultural, religious, or linguistic community] rights in subsection (1) may not be exercised in a manner inconsistent with any provision of the Bill of Rights" (Chapter 2, Section 31(2)).

Methods

Quantitative Analysis

Quantitative analyses of whether constitutional rights matter are fairly limited and have mixed results; quantitative studies of the effects of gender provisions for women's equality are even rarer. Some studies find that the impact of individual rights in the constitution on human rights is "somewhat discouraging" and that they have a limited impact on government behavior (Keith 2002, 134; Davenport 1996; Keith, Tate, and Poe 2009). Others find that democratic institutions and/or judicial independence are more important than individual rights provisions or are key conditions underlying the effectiveness of constitutional rights (Blasi and Cingranelli 1996; Cross 1999; Keith et al. 2009; Melton 2014).

Some quantitative studies are more optimistic about rights and their impact on a more narrowly defined set of outcomes. For example, Jeffords and Minkler (2016) examine the effect of environmental rights provisions in 198 countries and find that these rights are associated with higher environmental performance index scores. Matsuura (2019) has explored the effect of constitutional rights to health and found that health rights are associated with decreased infant mortality rates (but not a decrease in maternal mortality rates). With regard to gender provisions, our previous study found that egalitarian rights provisions in national constitutions were associated with higher scores on gender equality (Lambert and Scribner 2009), while Austen and Mavisakalyan (2016) find that constitutional protection from gender-based discrimination is associated with a larger percentage of women in parliament.

Chilton and Versteeg (2016, 2020) argue that some constitutional rights matter more than others. In particular, certain rights are more effective because they involve organizations interested in protecting these rights and can mobilize to punish governments that do not respect them. For example, they find that organizational rights such as the right to unionize and the right to establish political parties are "surprisingly effective," whereas individual rights such as freedom of expression and freedom of movement are less likely to have organized groups in place that can punish governments that trample rights and subsequently are less effective. In short, the presence of organized groups is an important factor in determining whether or not constitutional rights matter.

Similarly, the international law literature has emphasized the role played by organized groups. While some quantitative studies have found that international treaties do not matter or even have a negative impact (Hathaway 2002; Hafner-Burton and Tsutsui 2005; Keith 1999), others have argued that the mobilization of civil society, especially transnational advocacy networks, and/or democratic institutions are crucial for predicting whether human rights treaties will work (Neumayer 2005; Simmons 2009). Neumayer (2005), for example, finds that in non-democracies where civil society is often weak, ratification of human rights treaties has no effect. But ratification is associated with greater respect for human rights in more democratic countries with stronger civil society organizations.

Our statistical analysis adds to this literature. First, as noted earlier, our database is more comprehensive and nuanced than other attempts to code gender provisions. It allows us to test whether gender provisions have a measurable effect on women's equality across countries and over time. Specifically, we use the World Economic Forum's Gender Gap Index and its subindices that measure political, economic, health, and education outcomes for men and women as an indicator of gender equality across countries and over time. Our quantitative analysis uses the panel data from our database on constitutional provisions along with controls for political, economic, and institutional variables included in other quantitative analyses of constitutional provisions to test whether gender provisions are associated with higher WEF Gender Gap scores.

Second, we include measures of feminist mobilization in our analysis. As noted earlier, scholars have emphasized that if constitutional rights matter, their effect is conditioned by the presence of organized groups or a strong civil society; however, most quantitative studies have not tested for the strength or mobilization of rights organizations. In this study, we use Weldon's index of feminist mobilization as a key variable along with constitutional gender provisions. Weldon's index measures feminist mobilization across 126 countries over 40 years; this panel data overlaps well with our database of gender provisions.[13] Chapter 3 provides further details on the measures and statistical methods and presents the results of this analysis.

Quantitative analyses, like all methods, have limitations. They are not able to capture operations on the ground and thus cannot specify how constitutional provisions, in the hands of rights advocates, may contribute to political and social change. For this reason, we include two case studies that allow us to examine how advocates use gender provisions to secure legal change or defend prior gains that advance women's equality.

Case Studies

The case studies examine two pairs of countries in two regions that differ significantly with regard to gender provisions: Chile/Argentina and South Africa/Botswana. The case studies allow us to examine whether and how gender provisions impact processes and outcomes. The four countries are exposed to global and regional pressures to implement policies and create national gender machinery to improve the lives of women; each has well-developed (albeit increasingly fragmented) women's movements that are connected regionally and globally; and each faces conservative and traditional cultural forces in society, such as the Catholic Church in Latin America and the recognition of customary law in southern Africa. Cross-regionally, there are similarities related to the constitutionalization of gender equality. In South Africa and Argentina, constitutions were reformed as part of a democratic transition, and feminist activists were instrumental in the inclusion of a strong gender equality commitment in the constitution. In comparison, Botswana's and Chile's Constitutions are older and more conservative, and they do not go beyond a sex equality statement.[14]

The case studies combine interview and archival data on legislative and judicial outcomes. In each country, we conducted in-depth interviews with women's rights advocates in and out of government. We examine how rights advocates view and use the constitution and legislative and judicial outcomes between 1990 and 2020. We focus on efforts to secure legislative change and litigation strategies in three policy areas: gender-based violence, sexual and reproductive health, and employment rights. In the Botswana and South Africa case study, we also include customary and family law, a critical policy area in those countries. The case studies allow us to test whether constitutional provisions matter for process and outcomes regarding legitimacy, legislation, and litigation. Moreover, if constitutional provisions are important for women's rights advocacy in the ways outlined earlier, we might expect that women's rights advocates have more in common across regions than with their neighbors.

Notes

1 Tripp et al. (2009) and Banda (2005) make a similar point.
2 Customary law governs family law matters: marriage and divorce, rights within marriage, division of shared property, inheritance, and child custody. Customary laws consistently discriminate against and disadvantage women.
3 The South African Constitution guarantees wide access in Section 38(d), which makes "public interest" a ground on which a person may "approach a court."
4 See, for example, Center for Reproductive Rights (2005), Ewelukwa (2002), Scribner and Lambert (2010), and Ssenyonjo (2007).
5 Constitutions of the Countries of the World is a project of Oxford University Press.
6 Available at www.constituteproject.org.
7 The Global Gender Equality Constitutional Database is available at: https://constitutions.unwomen.org/en.
8 Details on scoring are presented in Chapter 3.
9 Countries in our database with neither a sex equality nor a gendered non-discrimination statement in their national constitution by 2015 are Australia, Costa Rica, Denmark, Egypt, France, Indonesia, Ireland, Israel, Jordan, Kuwait, Latvia, Lebanon, Monaco, Norway, Romania, Saudi Arabia, Seychelles, Singapore, Tonga, United States, Uruguay, and Yemen. Note: We only coded enumerated rights in the constitution. While France's preamble includes a principle of equality, its Constitution does not have a gender equality provision. However, Suk (2017) argues that this principle has constitutional status.
10 Many constitutions contain such a provision because it is one of the rights included in the Universal Declaration of Human Rights: "The family is the natural and fundamental group unit of society and is entitled to protection by society and the State" (Article 16, No. 3).
11 Law 19.611/1999, Act Amending the Constitution, established legal equality between men and women and the provision was revised to say, "all persons are born free and equal."

12 Legal pluralism exists when "two or more legal systems coexist in the same social field" (Merry 1988, 870). Customary, religious, traditional, or tribal laws and practices typically operate at a community level and may recognize the role of customary chiefs or local power-holders in dispute resolution.
13 Laurel Weldon, Feminist Mobilization Index. Available at: www.sfu.ca/politics/feministmovement.html.
14 An additional advantage is that these case studies offer comparisons of similarly situated countries with large differences in constitutions without the influence of the European Union and its directives. It also contributes to the comparative literature by focusing on non-European countries and regions.

References

Albertyn, Catherine R. 2019. "(In)equality and the South African Constitution." *Development Southern Africa* 36, no. 6: 751–766. DOI: 10.1080/0376835X.2019.1660860.

Albiston, Catherine R. and Gwendolyn M. Leachman. 2015. "Law as an Instrument of Social Change." In *International Encyclopedia of the Social & Behavioral Sciences*, second edition, edited by James D. Wright, 542–549. Oxford: Elsevier.

Andersen, Ellen Ann. 2009. *Out of the Closets and Into the Courts.* Ann Arbor: University of Michigan Press.

Austen, Sioban and Astghk Mavisakalyan. 2016. "Constitutions and the Political Agency of Women: A Cross-country Study." *Feminist Economics* 22, no. 1: 183–210.

Baines, Beverley and Ruth Rubio-Marin. 2005. "Introduction: Towards a Feminist Constitutional Agenda." In *The Gender of Constitutional Jurisprudence*, edited by Beverly Baines and Ruth Rubio-Marin, 1–21. Cambridge: Cambridge University Press.

Baldez, Lisa, Lee Epstein, and Andrew Martin. 2006. "Does the US Constitution Need an Equal Rights Amendment?" *Journal of Legal Studies* 35: 243–283.

Banda, Fareda. 2005. *Women, Law and Human Rights: An African Perspective.* Oxford and Portland, Oregon: Hart Publishing.

Blasi, Gerald J. and David Cingranelli. 1996. "Do Constitutions and Institutions Help Protect Human Rights?" In *Human Rights and Developing Countries*, edited by David Cingranelli, 4, 223–237.

Center for Reproductive Rights. 2005. *Legal Grounds: Reproductive and Sexual Rights in African Commonwealth Courts.* Toronto: Center for Reproductive Rights and the International Programme on Reproductive and Sexual Health Law at the University of Toronto. Available at: wp-content/uploads/2018/08/img_bo_legalgrounds.gif

Chilton, Adam S. and Mila Versteeg. 2016. "Do Constitutional Rights Make a Difference?" *American Journal of Political Science* 60, no. 3: 575–589.

Chilton, Adam S. and Mila Versteeg. 2020. *How Constitutional Rights Matter.* New York: Oxford University Press.

Craske, Nikki and Maxine Molyneux. 2002. "The Local, the Regional, and the Global: Transforming the Politics of Rights." In *Gender and the Politics of Rights and Democracy in Latin America*, edited by Nikki Craske and Maxine Molyneux, 1–31. New York: Palgrave Publishers Ltd.

Cross, Frank B. 1999. "The Relevance of Law in Human Rights Protection." *International Review of Law and Economics* 19, no. 1: 87–98.

Davenport, Christian A. 1996. "'Constitutional Promises' and Repressive Reality: A Cross-National Time-Series Investigation of Why Political and Civil Liberties Are Suppressed." *The Journal of Politics* 58, no. 3: 627–54.

De Fazio, Gianluca. 2012. "Legal Opportunity Structure and Social Movement Strategy in Northern Ireland and the Southern United States." *International Journal of Comparative Sociology* 53, no. 1: 3–22. DOI: 10.1177/0020715212439311.

Dobrowolsky, Alexandra and Vivien Hart. 2003. "Introduction: Women, New Politics and Constitutional Change." In *Women Making Constitutions: New Politics and Comparative Perspectives*, edited by Alexandra Dobrowolsky and Vivien Hart, 1–19. New York: Palgrave Macmillan.

Epp, Charles R. 1998. *The Rights Revolution: Lawyers, Activists, and Supreme Courts in Comparative Perspective*. Chicago and London: University of Chicago Press.

Ewelukwa, Uche U. 2002. "Post-Colonialism, Gender, Customary Injustice: Widows in African Societies." *Human Rights Quarterly* 24, no. 2: 424–486.

Fombad, Charles Manga. 2004. "The Constitutional Protection against Discrimination in Botswana." *International and Comparative Law Quarterly* 53: 139–170.

Ginsberg, Ruth Bader. 1979. "Sex Equality Under the 14th and Equal Rights Amendments." *Washington University Law Quarterly* 1979: 161–178.

Ginsburg, Tom and Aziz Huq. 2014. "What Can Constitutions Do? The Afghan Case." *Journal of Democracy* 25, no. 1: 116–130.

Goodman, Ryan and Derek Jinks. 2013. *Socializing States: Promoting Human Rights Through International Law*. New York: Oxford University Press.

Grugel, Jean and Enrique Peruzzotti. 2007. "Claiming Rights Under Global Governance: Children's Rights in Argentina." *Global Governance* 13: 199–216.

Grugel, Jean and Enrique Peruzzotti. 2012. "The Domestic Politics of International Human Rights Law: Implementing the Convention on the Rights of the Child in Ecuador, Chile, and Argentina." *Human Rights Quarterly* 34, no. 1: 178–198.

Hafner-Burton, Emilie and Kiyoteru Tsutsui. 2005. "Human Rights in a Globalizing World: The Paradox of Empty Promises." *American Journal of Sociology* 110, no. 5: 1373–1411.

Hafner-Burton, Emilie M., Brad L. LeVeck, and David G. Victor. 2016. "How Activists Perceive the Utility of International Law." *The Journal of Politics* 78, no. 1: 167–180.

Hathaway, Oona A. 2002. "Do Human Rights Treaties Make a Difference?" *The Yale Law Journal* 111, no. 8: 1935–2042.

Hilson, Chris. 2002. "New Social Movements: The Role of Legal Opportunity." *European Journal of Public Policy* 9, no. 2: 238–255.

Hirschl, Ran. 2004. *Towards Juristocracy: The Origins and Consequences of the New Constitutionalism*. Cambridge: Harvard University Press.

Hirschl, Ran and Sachar Ayelet. 2005. "Constitutional Transformation, Gender Equality, and Religious/National Conflict in Israel: Tentative Progress Through the Obstacle Course." In *The Gender of Constitutional Jurisprudence*, edited by Beverley Baines and Ruth Rubio-Marin, 205–229. Cambridge: Cambridge University Press.

Helen Irving. 2008. *Gender and the Constitution Equity and Agency in Comparative Constitutional Design*. New York: Cambridge University Press.

Hunter, Chris. 2006. "The Master's Tools Revisited: Can Law Contribute to Ending Violence Against Women?" *Institute Development Studies Bulletin* 37, no. 6: 57–68 (published February 8, 2016). https://doi.org/10.1111/j.1759-5436.2006.tb00323.x.

Jackson, Vicki. 2017. "Gender Equality Interpretation and Feminist Pluralism." In *Constitutions and Gender*, edited by Helen Irving, 221–251. Cheltenham: Edward Elgar Publishing.

Jagwanth, Saras and Christina Murray. 2005. "No Nation Can Be Free When Half of It Is Enslaved." In *The Gender of Constitutional Jurisprudence*, edited by Beverly Baines and Ruth Rubio-Marin, 230–255. Cambridge: Cambridge University Press.

Jeffords, Chris and Lanse Minkler. 2016. "Do Constitutions Matter? The Effects of Constitutional Environmental Rights Provisions on Environmental Outcomes." *Kyklos* 69, no. 2: 294–335.

Keck, Margaret and Kathryn Sikkink. 1998. *Activists Beyond Borders: Advocacy Networks in International Politics*. Ithaca: Cornell University Press.

Keith, Linda Camp. 1999. "The United Nations International Covenant on Civil and Political Rights: Does It Make a Difference in Human Rights Behavior?" *Journal of Peace Research* 36, no. 1: 95–118.

Keith, Linda Camp. 2002. "Constitutional Provisions for Individual Human Rights (1976–1996): Are They More Than Mere Window Dressing?" *Political Research Quarterly* 55: 111–143.

Keith, Linda Camp, C. Neal Tate, and Steven Poe. 2009. "Is the Law a Mere Parchment Barrier to Human Rights Abuse?" *The Journal of Politics* 71, no. 2: 644–660.

Lambert, Priscilla A. and Druscilla L. Scribner. 2009. "A Politics of Difference vs. a Politics of Equality: Do Constitutions Matter?" *Comparative Politics* 41, no. 3: 337–357.

Lambert Priscilla A. and Druscilla Scribner. 2020. "Constitutions and Women's Rights Advocacy: Strategic Uses of Gender Provisions in Argentina, Chile, Botswana, and South Africa." *Politics, Groups, and Identities* 8, no. 2: 228–247.

Lucas, Laura E. 2009. "Does Gender Specificity in Constitutions Matter." *Duke Journal of Comparative and International Law* 20: 133.

Matsuura, Hiroaki. 2019. "Exploring the Association Between the Constitutional Right to Health and Reproductive Outcomes in 157 Countries." *Sexual and Reproductive Health Matters* 27, no. 1: 168–180.

McCammon, Holly J. and Allison R. McGrath. 2015. "Litigating Change? Social Movements and the Court System." *Sociology Compass* 9, no. 2: 128–139.

McCann, Michael. 1994. *Rights at Work: Pay Equity Reform and the Politics of Legal Mobilization*. Chicago: University of Chicago Press.

Melton, James. 2014. "Do Constitutional Rights Matter?" unpublished paper. Available at: https://pdfs.semanticscholar.org/e030/faaef3401760e608dfb9faa13389bd41d377.pdf.

Merry, Sally Engle. 1988. "Legal Pluralism." *Law & Society Review* 22, no. 5: 869–896

Neumayer, Eric. 2005. "Do International Human Rights Treaties Improve Respect for Human Rights?" *Journal of Conflict Resolution* 49, no. 6: 925–953.

O'Sullivan, Michelle and Christina Murray. 2005. "Brooms Sweeping Oceans? Women's Rights in South Africa's First Decade of Democracy." *Acta Juridica* 17: 1–41.

Przeworski, Adam. 2004. "Institutions Matter?" *Government and Opposition* 39, no. 4: 527–540.

Rosenberg, Gerald. 1996. "Positivism, Interpretivism, and the Study of Law." *Law & Social Inquiry* 21, no. 1: 435–455.

Scheingold, Stuart A. 1974. *The Politics of Rights: Lawyers Public Policy and Political Change*. New Haven: Yale University Press.

Scheingold, Stuart A. 2004. *The Politics of Rights: Lawyers, Public Policy, and Political Change*, second edition. Ann Arbor: University of Michigan Press.

Scribner, Druscilla and Priscilla Lambert, 2010. "Constitutionalizing Difference: A Case Study Analysis of Gender Provisions in Botswana and South Africa." *Politics and Gender* 6, no. 1: 37–61.

Simmons, Beth. 2009. *Mobilizing for Human Rights: International Law in Domestic Politics*. Cambridge: Cambridge University Press.

Ssenyonjo, Manisuli. 2007. "Women's Rights to Equality and Non-Discrimination: Discriminatory Family Legislation in Uganda and the Role of Uganda's Constitutional Court." *International Journal of Law, Policy and the Family* 21, no. 3: 341–372.

Strauss, David. 2001. "The Irrelevance of Constitutional Amendments." *Harvard Law Review* 90: 1457–1505.
Suk, Julie C. 2017. "An Equal Rights Amendment for the Twenty-First Century: Bringing Global Constitutionalism Home." *Yale Journal of Law & Feminism* 28: 381–444.
Tripp, Aili Mari, Isabel Casimiro, Joy Kwesiga, and Alice Mungwa. 2009. *African Women's Movements: Transforming Political Landscapes*. Cambridge: Cambridge University Press.
Tsutsui, Kiyoteru, Claire Whitlinger, and Alwin Lim. 2012. "International Human Rights Law and Social Movements." *Annual Review of Law and Social Sciences* 8: 367–396
UN Women. 2017. "Why and How Constitutions Matter for Advancing Gender Equality." *Policy Brief* 8. Available at: https://www.unwomen.org/en/digital-library/publications/2017/2/why-and-how-constitutions-matter-for-advancing-gender-equality
Vanhala, Lisa. 2017. "Is Legal Mobilization for the Birds? Legal Opportunity Structures and Environmental Nongovernmental Organizations in the United Kingdom, France, Finland, and Italy." *Comparative Political Studies* 51, no. 3: 380–412. DOI: doi.org/10.1177/0010414017710257.
Waylen, Georgina. 2007. "Women's Mobilization and Gender Outcomes in Transitions to Democracy: The Case of South Africa." *Comparative Political Studies* 40, no. 5: 521–546.
Williams, Susan. 2009. "Introduction: Comparative Constitutional Law, Gender Equality, and Constitutional Design." In *Constituting Equality: Gender Equality and Comparative Constitutional Law*, edited by Susan Williams, 1–28. Cambridge: Cambridge University Press.

3

CONSTITUTIONAL GENDER PROVISIONS AND EQUALITY

Cross-National Evidence

Priscilla A. Lambert, Druscilla L. Scribner and J. Kevin Corder

Introduction

In this chapter, we use our database of constitutional gender provisions and our related typology of constitutional provisions as egalitarian, maternal, or neutral to explore the relationship between gender rights provisions and gender equality outcomes. Do provisions that obligate the state to attend to women's health result in better health outcomes? Does constitutional recognition of affirmative action support greater economic equality? Is the gap between men and women in the political sphere smaller in countries where women's equality is constitutionally valued, protected, and promoted? Conversely, where constitutional values and rights prioritize traditional gender roles, are the gaps between women's and men's social or political power wider?

We consider mid-range legislative outcomes and long-range gender equality outcomes. Constitutional rights may help advocates remove discriminatory legislation and may even help them push for more progressive laws that promote women's ability to enjoy the same opportunities as men. Thus, we look at whether specific rights and provisions are associated with a more women-friendly legal framework. These legal frameworks may, in turn, contribute to greater gender equality. We also examine whether constitutional provisions, along with other explanatory factors, contribute to gender equality as measured by global indicators.

We begin by examining laws and legal protections relative to the presence or absence of the constitutional rights most closely tied to these policy outcomes. We observe a pattern in which countries with egalitarian constitutional rights are more likely to have stronger legal frameworks supporting women's rights. We then turn to our panel data analysis, beginning with an overview of gender

DOI: 10.4324/9781003303725-3

equality across countries and time using the World Economic Forum's (WEF's) Global Gender Gap Index and our scores for egalitarian and maternal constitutional provisions. In the last section, we present a cross-national statistical analysis of the relationship between constitutional provisions and gender equality from 1995 to 2015. This approach allows us to sort out the potential effects of different kinds of provisions on gender equality while controlling for other important explanatory factors. In the panel data analysis, we find that egalitarian provisions are associated with higher scores for the Global Gender Gap Index and its component subindices, while maternal provisions are negatively associated with these scores.

Gender Provisions and Mid-Range Outcomes

We use our constitutional database, described in Chapters 1 and 2, to explore possible relationships between gender provisions and mid-range outcomes such as legislation supporting women's equality with men and social indicators that capture gender-based disparities. In this section, we examine the relationships between specific types of gender provisions and related laws in four key policy areas: gender-based violence, reproductive health, workplace equality, and customary law.

If constitutional provisions do impact outcomes, we expect it will take some time for that effect to manifest itself in laws or indicators that capture women's legal status. For this reason, we look at gender provisions in constitutions in the year 2005, while our measures of laws and equality are dated 2019. To assure consistency with comparative cross-national data, we rely on the OECD's Gender, Institutions and Development Database (GID-DB) 2019. This database is one of the most comprehensive regarding the number of countries, gender-related laws, and gender equality indicators covered.

The GID-DB incorporates data from the OECD's Social Institutions and Gender Index (SIGI), which is a cross-national measure of gender-based discrimination in social institutions (formal and informal laws, social norms, and practices).[1] The SIGI measures the legal framework on a scale of 0–1, where 0 indicates that the legal framework ensures women's full legal equality or full legal protection and 1 indicates that women do not enjoy the same rights as men or receive no protection. Importantly for this study, the indices for legal frameworks measure the presence of laws and legislation rather than constitutional rights. This section focuses on simple comparisons and associations. The results are suggestive of the possible relationship between provisions and legislative outcomes. They do not indicate causality, nor do they take into account the many other factors that contribute to the variation in legal frameworks. Moreover, some of the most progressive provisions appear in only a handful of constitutions. With these caveats in mind, we can look for observable patterns in the data in the four policy areas.

Gender-Based Violence Provisions

Constitutional provisions related to gender-based violence include a right to security of the person and/or a right to bodily integrity, as well as gender-specific language about freedom from violence. Following the Universal Declaration of Human Rights, many constitutions include a gender-neutral right to security of the person or bodily integrity. Thirty percent of the countries in our database did so at each time point. There has been a slow but steady increase in the number of constitutions that include gender-specific provisions on the right to be free from violence, from 4 out of 100 in 1995 to 21 out of 164 in 2015. Ecuador's Constitution has perhaps the most comprehensive approach to gender-based violence[2] (and other forms of violence). For example, Article 66, Section 3, the right to personal well-being, guarantees the following:

66.3.a Bodily, psychological, moral, and sexual safety.

66.3.b A life without violence in the public and private sectors. The State shall adopt the measures needed to prevent, eliminate, and punish all forms of violence, especially violence against women, children, and adolescents, elderly persons, persons with disabilities, and against all persons at a disadvantage or in a vulnerable situation.

Figure 3.1 summarizes the SIGI scores of the legal framework that protects (or fails to protect) women from gender-based violence compared to our related constitutional database measures. The pattern here is that the presence of gender-neutral rights to bodily integrity and/or freedom from violence is associated with a slightly better legal framework than no recognition of these rights. Gender-specific statements are associated with greater legal protection, and women are the most protected in the few countries where the state is obligated to act.

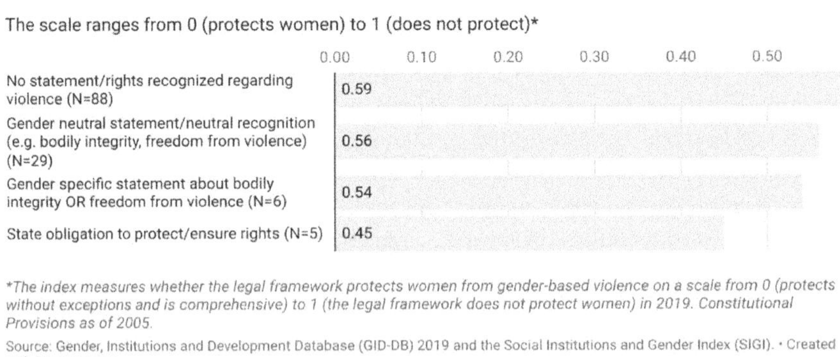

FIGURE 3.1 Gender-based violence provisions and the legal framework protecting women from gender-based violence

Reproductive Rights Provisions

The right to determine whether and how many children to have is often left to statutory law. However, about half of national constitutions include provisions that guarantee access to health care, which can impact access to reproductive health care services. Constitutional rights to family planning services and/or reproductive health care are unusual, but their number is gradually increasing over time. Abortion bans are very rare in national constitutions, but some countries include a right to life of the unborn (e.g., Ireland) or a right to life from conception (e.g., Chile).[3]

A handful of constitutions specify both rights to family planning or reproductive healthcare services and the right to life of the unborn. Turning again to Ecuador's Constitution, we find extensive guarantees of reproductive autonomy: Article 66, Sections 9 and 10 guarantee the right to make decisions about one's sexuality and sexual life and the right to make "responsible and informed decisions about one's health and reproductive life and to decide how many children to have"; Article 332 ensures social and labor rights for pregnant and nursing women; and Article 32 promises that:

> 32 Health is a right guaranteed by the State . . . The State shall guarantee this right by . . . access to programs, actions and services promoting and providing integral healthcare, sexual health, and reproductive health. The provision of healthcare services shall be governed by the principles of equity, universality, . . . with a gender and generational approach.

At the same time, the Constitution has a provision that guarantees the right to life from conception.

Figure 3.2 shows the average SIGI scores of the legal framework for reproductive autonomy relative to reproductive rights in the constitution. Countries

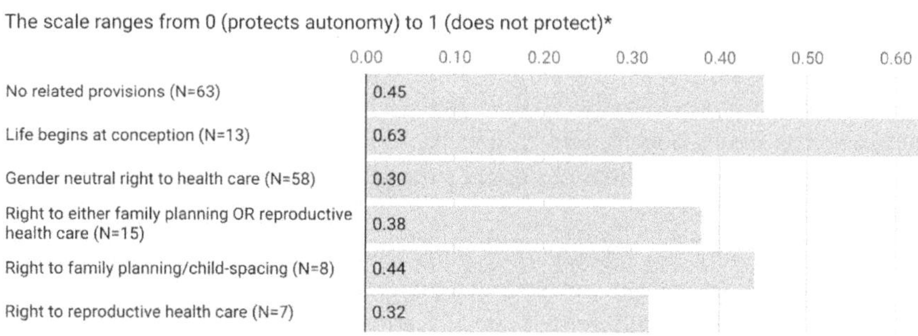

**The index measures whether the legal framework protects women's reproductive health and rights in case of unwanted pregnancy on a scale from 0 (protects without any justifications) to 1 (does not protect women's reproductive health and rights in case of unwanted pregnancy) in 2019. Constitutional provisions as of 2005.*

Source: Gender, Institutions and Development Database (GID-DB) 2019 and the Social Institutions and Gender Index (SIGI). • Created with Datawrapper

FIGURE 3.2 Sexual and reproductive health provisions and legal reproductive autonomy

that constitutionally recognize that life begins at conception have the least protective legal framework for reproductive autonomy, followed by countries with no right to health care. These countries score closer to 1 on the SIGI index, which indicates no legal protection. Fifteen constitutions had either a right to family planning or a right to reproductive health in 2005. If we look at these two rights separately, the right to family planning is not associated with greater protection than those countries with no provisions, but the right to reproductive health care is. Overall, the strongest legal framework for reproductive autonomy is associated with constitutional rights to health care generally and reproductive health care specifically. As noted earlier, three of the countries (including Ecuador) that enumerate significant reproductive rights also have an anti-abortion statement. The latter is a significant hurdle to legislating reproductive health rights and counters the potential impact of a reproductive health rights provision.

Workplace Protection and Equality Provisions

In the economic arena, constitutional provisions can be more or less egalitarian or maternal. We categorized provisions recognizing workplace equality and equal pay for equal work statements as egalitarian in the database. For example, Ghana's Constitution includes multiple statements regarding workplace equality, including equality of opportunity, equal rights to training and promotion, and childcare so that women "can realize their full potential" (Articles 27 and 36).

Provisions emphasizing the need to protect women, especially pregnant women, fall into our maternal category. Slovakia's Constitution does not have egalitarian provisions for equal pay for equal work or equal opportunity in the workplace. Yet, it does specify that "Women, minors, and disabled persons have a right to more extensive health protection and special working conditions" (Article 38, Section 1). It also ensures that pregnant women are "entitled to special treatment, terms of employment, and working conditions" (Article 41, Section 2). We expect maternal provisions in general to negatively impact the passage of women-friendly laws, as captured in the SIGI workplace legal framework. Some protective measures may have a positive effect, however, if the underlying assumption is that with such protections, women can better participate in the economic and political arenas (Suk 2018, 153).

Figure 3.3 shows the average SIGI score on the workplace legal framework by constitutional provisions concerning equal pay for equal work and workplace protection. Countries with gender-specific equal pay for equal work provisions are associated with slightly stronger legal frameworks. Concerning protective provisions, the workplace legal framework score does not vary greatly. Still, the legal framework is more likely to guarantee equality between men and women where constitutions include gendered workplace protection provisions that obligate state action or enforcement.

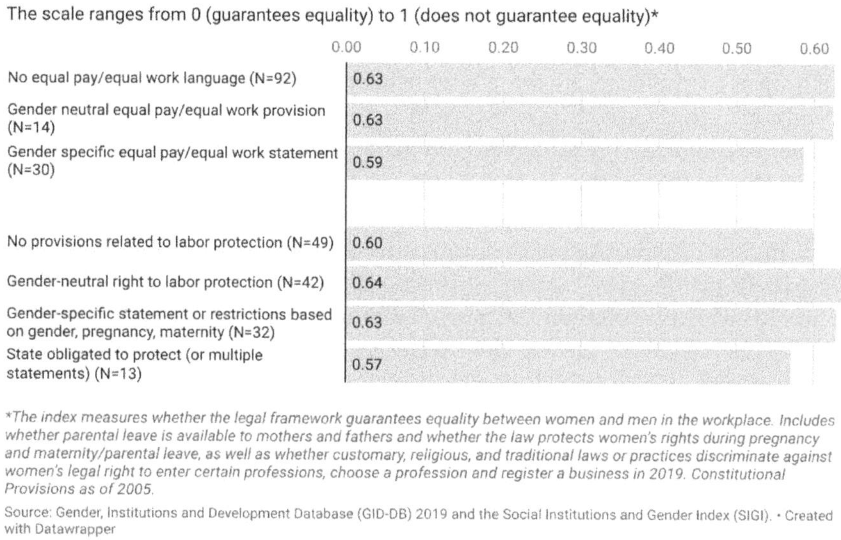

FIGURE 3.3 Workplace equality and protection provisions and legal framework for workplace equality

Family and Customary Law Provisions

Family law regulates matters such as marriage, divorces, child custody, spousal support, and property rights related to inheritance. As discussed in Chapter 2, in some countries, customary law may substitute for received family law; thus, the relationship between individual rights and custom affects the legal framework for women entering into and leaving a marriage and their property rights during and after marriage and in relationship to other family members. While most of our constitutions did not mention customary law or its constitutional status (87 do not), the remaining 49 constitutions in 2005 did. Of those, nine constitutions exempted customary law from constitutional rights. For example, the non-discrimination provision in Section 6 of the Constitution of Sierra Leone states, "Subject to the provisions of subsection (4), (5), and (7), no law shall make provision which is discriminatory either of itself or in its effect." However, subsection (4) exempts this right when the law in question is custom or personal law. Botswana has a similar provision. Chapter 5 demonstrates how these exemptions, sometimes called clawback clauses, interfere with sex equality or non-discrimination statements that may appear in the constitution and impede advocates' ability to fight against discriminatory laws and practices.

In 22 of the constitutions, customary rights were recognized, but the relationship to other constitutional rights is ambiguous. Vanuatu's Constitution is a good example: "Customary law shall continue to have effect as part of the law of the Republic of Vanuatu" (Article 95, No. 3). This ambiguity leaves any constitutional rights open to challenges by those who benefit from customary law, and consequently, it is expected to impact women's rights negatively. In contrast, a similar number of countries (18) recognize customary and cultural rights but specify that these rights are limited by the individual rights enumerated in the constitution. South Africa's Constitution includes such a provision, as does Peru's now and in 2005. In Peru, "Authorities of rural and native communities, in conjunction with the peasant patrols, may exercise jurisdictional functions at the territorial level in accordance with common law, provided they do not violate the fundamental rights of the individual" (Article 149). We expect that such statements will provide advocates with tools to fight discriminatory customary practices.

Figures 3.4 and 3.5 examine constitutional provisions related to equality within marriage and the constitutional status of customary law with respect to the legal framework affecting women's ability to divorce and inherit land or other assets. To guarantee that women enjoy equal rights in marriage and family law, Japan's Constitution ensures that:

> 24 Marriage shall be based only on the mutual consent of both sexes and it shall be maintained through mutual cooperation with the equal rights of husband and wife as a basis.
>
> With regard to choice of spouse, property rights, inheritance, choice of domicile, divorce and other matters pertaining to marriage and the family, laws shall be enacted from the standpoint of individual dignity and the essential equality of the sexes.

Figure 3.4 shows that the legal framework for women's equality in divorce, inheritance, and property is much stronger where constitutional provisions specify marital equality. There are also clear and substantial differences concerning the

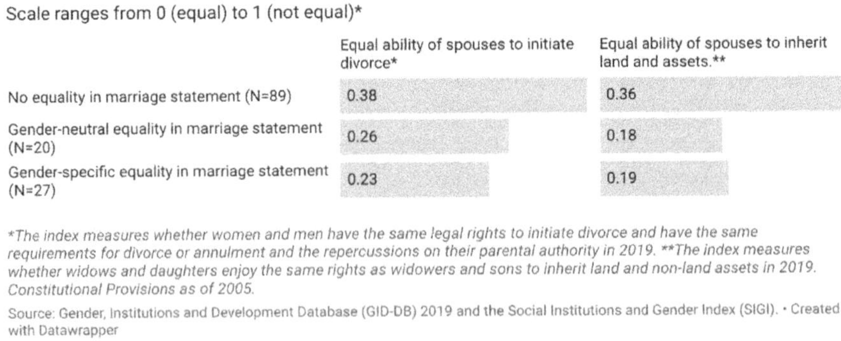

FIGURE 3.4 Marital equality provisions and legal framework for equality

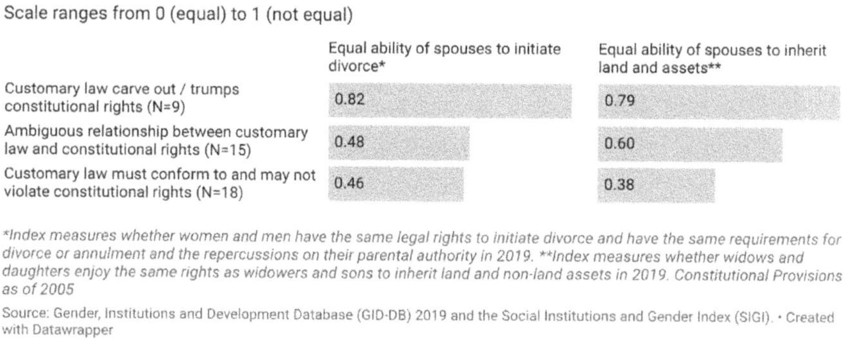

FIGURE 3.5 Constitutional recognition of customary law and the legal framework for equality

constitutional position of customary law, with much stronger protections for women's equal ability to initiate divorce and to inherit or own property in countries where customary law is subordinate to constitutional rights to equality. This is evident in Figure 3.5.

The statistics summarized in this section are descriptive, sometimes based on a small number of countries, and do not account for factors other than constitutional provisions that may also be associated with the legal framework. The rest of this chapter aims to assess whether constitutional rights are associated with women's equality and welfare when taking into account other explanations and standard controls used in quantitative analyses of constitutional rights. We describe and summarize our main dependent and independent variables in the following section and then turn to the statistical analysis.

Multivariate Analysis

Measuring Gender Equality

The WEF's Gender Gap Index provides a comparative measure of a country's proximity to achieving the goal of gender equality (on a scale of 0–1, where women's full equality with men equals 1). The Gender Gap Index, first reported in 2006, quantifies the gap between outcomes for men and women in 156 countries in four key areas: economic participation and opportunity, educational attainment, health and survival, and political empowerment.[4] The WEF publishes an aggregate Gender Gap measure and subindex measures for each country annually.[5] In 2006, the Gender Gap Index ranged from 0.8133 (Sweden) to 0.4594 (Yemen). In 2021, the Gender Gap Index ranged from 0.892 (Iceland) to 0.444 (Afghanistan). During this period, the average score for the countries in our database increased from 0.663 in 2006 to 0.707 in 2021. The gap between women and men narrowed in this 15-year period.

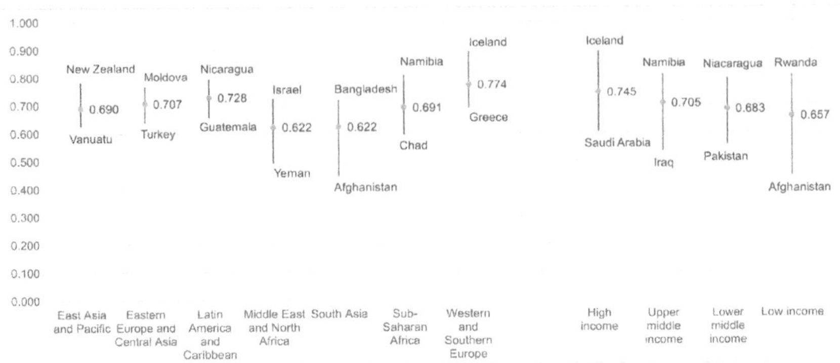

FIGURE 3.6 World Economic Forum 2021 Global Gender Gap scores by world region and income group

Figure 3.6 shows the average Global Gender Gap scores and the range of scores across regions and by income group. Not surprisingly, the gap is narrowest in European countries and highest in countries in the MENA and South Asian regions. By income group, women are more likely to enjoy greater equality in wealthier countries (on average), but the top scores in all the other income groups are nearly even. This indicates that the level of development matters but is not decisive. Less developed and low-income countries have reduced the gap in outcomes between women and men, and many low- and middle-income countries outperform the average score in high-income countries. We use the Global Gender Gap Index and the political empowerment, economic participation, and health and survival subindices as dependent variables. Summary statistics for the subindices appear in the Appendix at the end of the chapter. Regionally, there is considerable variation, except in the health and survival index (Appendix Table 1).[6]

Egalitarian, Maternal, and Gender-Neutral Provisions

In Chapters 1 and 2, we laid out a typology of constitutional gender provisions with three types of provisions: gender-neutral, corresponding to a formal equality framework; egalitarian, approximating a substantive equality approach concerned with removing or overcoming gender-based barriers to equality; and maternal, which reveres and reinforces women's maternal and caregiving roles.

Our cross-national database codes for the presence of each type of provision and for state obligations to act, focusing on three points in time: 1995, 2005, and 2015. Twelve of the coding questions measure egalitarian provisions. These questions relate to sex equality statements, non-discrimination provisions, equal political participation directives, equal citizenship, equal suffrage, gender quotas, marital equality, reproductive health rights, gender-based violence, equal pay for equal work, workplace equality, and family leave. Five coding questions specifically relate to the degree to which the constitution provides special protections or rights for families, mothers, and pregnant women and obligates state action in these areas. These provisions include those concerned with family protection, maternity leave, workplace protection based on gender, pregnancy or maternity, social rights directed at women as mothers specifically, and any special treatment that categorizes women with minors and the disabled. High scores in these areas indicate a strong constitutional commitment to protecting and supporting women's maternal and familial roles. Recall that gender-neutral constitutions emphasize individual rights and equal treatment and do not recognize gender differences or a need for special treatment of women. Low scores on all these questions indicate a gender-neutral approach or the absence of rights. In creating the egalitarian and maternal scores, we scored each provision a one if there is a gender-specific right in the constitution and a two if it also specifies that the state had an obligation to ensure the right was implemented or if there were multiple statements. For example, South Africa scores a 2 on reproductive rights because its Constitution includes multiple statements about reproductive rights under the sections on health care and social security and again under freedom and security of the person (Chapter 2, Sections 12 and 27); it also includes language about the state's obligation to provide services and ensure access.

Table 3.1 shows the change over time in the egalitarian and maternal scores by region for the 100 countries for which we have data for all three time points. In nearly every region and income group, the average score for egalitarian provisions has increased. This result is consistent with research that documents a global tendency to include a broad array of rights, including socioeconomic, environmental, and even animal rights (Law and Versteeg 2011; Elkins, Ginsburg, and Simmons 2013). It also reflects the fact that constitutional conventions and amendment processes have become more inclusive. The presence of women at the table is associated with many more gender rights in the constitution (Albertyn 2017; Dobrowolsky and Hart 2003; Irving 2008).

The highest egalitarian scores can be found in the Latin America/Caribbean region, South Asia, and Sub-Saharan Africa,[7] while the Middle East/North Africa and East Asia/Pacific regions have the lowest scores on egalitarian provisions. Maternal provisions are most common in Eastern Europe/Central Asia and Latin America/Caribbean, but few countries have added new or stronger maternal provisions since 1995. By income group, the number of egalitarian provisions is considerably higher in less economically developed countries. These countries have newer constitutions influenced in part by the adoption of human rights conventions, including the CEDAW. In contrast, the wealthiest countries are much less likely to include gender provisions of any sort.

Overall, we expect that egalitarian constitutional provisions will positively impact women's social, economic, and political status for the reasons outlined in Chapter 2. Egalitarian provisions enable advocacy by providing legal tools and lending legitimacy to efforts to seek policy change through the legislature or the courts. If constitutional gender provisions facilitate rights advocates' ability

TABLE 3.1 Average egalitarian and maternal constitutional provision scores by region and income, 1995–2015

	1995		*2005*		*2015*	
	Egalitarian	*Maternal*	*Egalitarian*	*Maternal*	*Egalitarian*	*Maternal*
Anglo Countries	1.40	0.00	1.60	0.00	1.60	0.00
East Asia and the Pacific	1.50	0.75	1.50	0.81	1.56	0.81
Eastern Europe and Central Asia	2.25	4.00	2.63	4.50	2.63	4.38
Latin America and the Caribbean	3.83	3.61	4.04	3.61	5.17	3.65
The Middle East and North Africa	0.43	2.57	0.43	2.57	1.00	2.86
South Asia	4.00	2.40	4.20	2.40	6.40	2.60
Sub-Saharan Africa	5.50	2.19	5.69	2.19	5.88	2.19
Western and Southern Europe	2.35	1.65	3.10	1.85	3.20	1.95
Low income	7.67	3.00	7.67	3.00	7.67	3.00
Lower middle income	3.18	2.68	3.36	2.68	4.43	2.79
Upper middle income	2.96	2.57	3.04	2.75	3.61	2.79
High income	2.03	1.58	2.58	1.68	2.61	1.71
Mean	2.95	2.25	3.23	2.34	3.70	2.39
S.D.	2.88	2.19	2.92	2.17	3.41	2.20

to secure better legislation and judicial outcomes, this outcome should generally promote women's equality. Of course, many other factors are at play in this potential chain of events; we discuss these factors in the next section. We hypothesize that *countries with more egalitarian provisions will have closed more of the gender gap than countries with few egalitarian rights.*

Maternal provisions emphasize and tend to reinforce women's reproductive and maternal roles and are more likely to facilitate policies that protect or differentiate women from men. Ultimately, such provisions may exercise a negative effect because they often reinforce traditional gender roles. We hypothesize that *countries with mostly maternal provisions will have a larger gender gap than countries with egalitarian provisions or even countries with neutral provisions.*

Alternative Explanations and Control Variables

Drawing on the quantitative research on the effect of constitutional rights and human rights treaties on government repression or rights abuses, we identify several factors in addition to gender provisions that may help explain variations in the gender gap across countries and over time. Specifically, we include women's mobilization, regime type, and several controls regularly included in these studies.[8]

Only a limited number of quantitative studies have examined the effects of constitutional rights, and quantitative analyses of the effects of gender provisions on women's equality are even rarer. Many quantitative studies have found that constitutional rights and human rights treaties have little or no effect. Those that do find a positive effect argue that it depends on the presence of other factors, such as the level of democracy, judicial independence, or the strength of civil society and organized citizen groups (Chilton and Versteeg 2020; Crabtree and Nelson 2017; Keith 2002; Keith, Tate and Poe 2009; Metelska-Szaniawska and Lewkowicz 2021; Melton 2014; Neumayer 2005). Several quantitative and most qualitative studies find that the mobilization of citizen groups is essential. However, few quantitative studies on constitutional rights have included measures of the strength of civil society in their models.[9] Our analysis includes a measure for women's mobilization and helps to fill this gap in the literature.

Women's Mobilization

In quantitative studies of the impact of constitutional rights, scholars have found that some rights are easier to enforce when organized groups (e.g., religious organizations or unions) are already in a position to use the constitution to protect these rights against government infringement (Chilton and Versteeg 2016, 2020). The transnational advocacy literature also finds that human rights treaties are more likely to have an impact when transnational advocacy networks or civil society groups are strong (Hafner-Burton and Tsutsui 2005; Neumayer 2005; Simmons 2009; Tsutsui et al. 2012).

Comparative and feminist studies have also pointed to the role that women's movements play. In many countries, for example, the women's movement and issue-specific feminist organizations have played a crucial role in crafting, achieving, and monitoring policy change in key areas, such as the adoption of electoral quotas and legislative reform.[10] Similarly, Weldon (2002) and Htun and Weldon (2012, 2018) have argued that the strength and autonomy of feminist movements are important for explaining the variation in gender policy (particularly violence against women legislation).

In short, unless rights advocates use the rights enumerated in the constitutions, these provisions are likely to remain "window dressing" or "empty promises" (Keith 2002; Hafner Burton and Tsutsui 2005). Thus, the role of feminist organizations is critical: they can take up the legal tools offered by constitutional rights to reverse discriminatory practices and advocate for the expansion of women's rights. We include Weldon's index of feminist mobilization provisions to examine how women's agency is related to the gender gap across countries. Weldon's Feminist Mobilization Index (FMI) ranges from 0 to 3, where a 0 indicates no significant feminist mobilization and a 3 indicates a strong and autonomous feminist movement that is an important promoter of policy change. The FMI codes for the strength and autonomy of feminist mobilization in 126 countries at five points in time: 1975, 1985, 1995, 2005, and 2015.[11] We hypothesize that a strong and autonomous feminist movement will be positively associated with a higher score on the Gender Gap score.

Democracy and Constitution Age

Stable democratic institutions are associated with better rights practices and are regularly included in quantitative studies on the effect of constitutional provisions and human rights treaties. The level of democracy also matters for gender equality. Liberal (constitutional) democracy protects and extends the individual rights necessary for political engagement and policy change. Beer (2009) finds that long-term democracy, which is often accompanied by the social and cultural changes that come with modernization, plays a significant role in improving the status of women relative to men. These changes may be more strongly associated with democracy than the level of economic development: "While modernization and economic development are clearly important in generating greater gender equality, long-term democracy and women's participation in democracy are also strongly related to greater gender equality" (Beer 2009, 226). We follow common practice and use Polity 2 from the Polity IV dataset to gauge the level of democracy, and we hypothesize that more democratic countries will have higher levels of gender equality.[12]

We also use the duration or age of the constitution as a control because newer regimes are more likely to adopt new constitutional rights, known as the imitation effect. These regimes are also less likely to have well-established rights practices (Law and Versteeg 2013; Elkins et al. 2013).

Judicial Independence

Several studies have found that the effect of constitutional rights depends upon judicial independence (Blasi and Cingranelli 1996; Keith, Tate, and Poe 2009; Melton 2014). An independent judiciary increases the likelihood that human rights violations will be punished and has been linked to better rights protection and even enforcement (Keith 2002; Melton 2014; Keith et al. 2009). Thus, judicial independence is regularly included in quantitative analyses of constitutions and human rights treaties. Following common practice, we use Cingranelli and Richards' index of judicial independence from the CIRI dataset as a control variable.[13]

Socio-Economic Development and Population

In nations with higher levels of economic development and per-capita income, women usually enjoy more opportunities to pursue post-secondary education, participate in the paid labor force, and engage in political activity. Economic modernization is also typically associated with lower fertility rates, greater urbanization, and changing attitudes about the role of women in society. As seen in Figure 3.6, the higher the income group, the higher the average gender gap score. We expect higher levels of economic development to be associated with greater levels of gender equality. Accordingly, we include GDP per capita as reported by the World Bank as a control variable. Population size is also a standard control variable in most quantitative studies of constitutions and human rights treaties; there is mixed evidence that rights abuses are more common in large countries.[14]

Panel Regressions

There are 100 countries for which we have constitutions and measures of our dependent and independent variables at three time points (1995, 2005, and 2015); for 2005 and 2015, we have data on 136 and 164 countries, respectively. The estimates are based on OLS with panel-corrected standard errors. We use year-fixed effects to account for improvements in the Gender Gap Index over time and country-fixed effects to account for national-level differences not included in the model that may explain outcomes. The models reported here evaluate how constitutional provisions affect the WEF's aggregate Gender Gap measure and the subindices measuring gender gaps in political empowerment, economic participation, and health and survival about five years later.[15] They include controls for feminist mobilization, democratic institutions (rule of law, government effectiveness), economic development (per capita GDP), and the age of the constitution (duration). The standard errors are adjusted to account for heteroskedasticity (robust standard errors).

Table 3.2 presents the panel regression results with the WEF Gender Gap Index as the dependent variable. Although the country-fixed effects explain a great deal

TABLE 3.2 Panel regression results. Dependent variable = Global Gender Gap Index

	1	*2*	*3*	*4*
Egalitarian	0.004***	0.004***	0.003***	0.004***
	(0.001)	(0.001)	(0.001)	(0.001)
Maternal	−0.002	−0.008**	−0.005**	−0.008**
	(0.003)	(0.003)	(0.002)	(0.003)
Customary law	0.002	0.003	0.003	0.002
	(0.004)	(0.004)	(0.004)	(0.004)
Feminist mobilization		0.003	0.002	0.003
		(0.004)	(0.004)	(0.004)
Polity 2		−0.003***		−0.003***
		(0.001)		(0.001)
Judicial independence			−0.001	−0.001
			(0.005)	(0.005)
Age of constitution		−0.006***	−0.004	−0.006***
		(0.002)	(0.002)	(0.002)
GDP (logged)		−0.005	−0.006	−0.005
		(0.006)	(0.006)	(0.006)
Population (logged)		0.016	0.002	0.015
		(0.019)	(0.018)	(0.019)
Year = 2010	0.017***	0.079***	0.061***	0.078***
	(0.003)	(0.014)	(0.014)	(0.015)
Year = 2020	0.041***	0.161***	0.124***	0.160***
	(0.004)	(0.027)	(0.028)	(0.029)
N	319	250	252	248
Adjusted R-squared	0.919	0.912	0.905	0.912

Notes: ***$p<0.01$, **$p<0.05$, and *$p<0.1$. Country-fixed effects are not shown.

of the variation in the gender gap, the estimates of the constitutional provisions are consistent: egalitarian provisions are associated with higher WEF Gender Gap scores overall, while maternal provisions are not—rather they are associated with lower scores. The customary law provisions are positive but not significant in most of our estimates. Only about a third of our constitutions mention customary law, so it is not surprising that this result is not statistically significant. However, it is important to keep customary provisions in the model because they can (and do) undermine provisions guaranteeing equality or non-discrimination; or, in the constitutions that specify that customary law is subordinate to individual rights, they reinforce egalitarian provisions.

The size of the effects of constitutional provisions is not trivial. The range of the egalitarian provisions is from −1 to 16. Thus, a change from the lowest score to the highest egalitarian score implies a change of 0.004 × 17 or 0.068 in the Gender Gap Index score. The standard deviation for the overall Gender Gap Index is 0.061, so the Gender Gap Index moves up by over a full standard deviation across the range of the egalitarian score. In contrast, for maternal provisions, which range from 0 to 8, a change from the lowest to the highest maternal score corresponds to a decrease in the Gender Gap score of -0.008×8 or -0.064.

Table 3.3 presents regression results with the Gender Gap subindices for health and survival, economic empowerment, and political empowerment as the dependent variables. In these estimates, egalitarian provisions are once again positive, and maternal provisions are negative. The coefficient for maternal provisions is larger and statistically significant in the case of economic empowerment and political empowerment, but not for health and survival. This confirms our suspicion that maternal provisions may help protect and improve women's well-being to some degree, but the emphasis on women's roles as mothers and caregivers negatively impacts their ability to gain equality in the paid labor force or the halls of power. For example, in a country with the highest score on maternal provisions, the political empowerment subindex, which is measured by the percent of women in parliament, in ministries, and years with a female head of state, decreases by -0.016×8 or -0.128, or almost the equivalent to the standard deviation for the political empowerment score (0.157).

Robustness Checks

One concern with these results is that some of the control variables do not have the expected sign. This is probably due to the fact that GDP, polity scores, and judicial independence are correlated with each other. However, a correlation matrix did not show correlations large enough to warrant any remedial action. The most highly correlated variables were polity 2 and judicial independence ($r = 0.56$) and polity and GDP ($r = 0.47$), so we ran regressions dropping first polity and then judicial independence scores, but the regression estimates were very similar (see Table 3.2). That is, additional controls do not change the sign of the coefficients for the constitutional provisions (although in some cases, they change from significant to not significant).

As noted earlier, the lags between the year when constitutional provision scores are calculated and the Gender Gap Index are not consistent. To see how robust the estimates are to changing the length of time between adoption and measurement of the gender gap, we ran two separate regressions: the first set of estimates uses year 2005 and 2015 constitutional provision scores with Gender Gap outcomes in 2010 and 2020 (five-year lags), and the second set uses 1995 and 2005 provisions predicting 2006 and 2020 Gender Gap outcomes (11–15-year lags). This requires dropping about a third of the sample in both regressions—the set of observations with 1995 constitutional provisions and 2015 provisions, respectively. While some variables were no longer significant, the signs of the coefficients did not change (results not shown).

TABLE 3.3 Panel regression results for subindices measuring the gender gap in health and survival, economic participation and opportunity, and political empowerment

	DV = Health Gap	*DV = Health Gap*	*DV = Econ. Gap*	*DV = Econ. Gap*	*DV = Political Gap*	*DV = Political Gap*
Egalitarian	0.0004	0.001*	0.003	0.006*	0.007	0.004
	(0.0003)	(0.0003)	(0.003)	(0.003)	(0.004)	(0.004)
Maternal	−0.001)	−0.001	−0.004	−0.011**	−0.002	−0.016**
		(0.001)	(0.005)	(0.005)	(0.010)	(0.008)
Customary law	0.002*	0.001	0.013*	0.010	0.008	0.018
	(0.001)	(0.001)	(0.007)	(0.008)	(0.016)	(0.015)
Feminist mobilization		−0.002**		0.005		0.007
		(0.001)		(0.009)		(0.013)
Polity 2		−0.0004*		−0.004		−0.008**
		(0.002)		(0.003)		(0.003)
Judicial independence		0.002		0.003		−0.001
		(0.001)		(0.009)		(0.015)
Age of constitution		−0.001***		−0.014***		−0.003
		(0.0004)		(0.004)		(0.005)
GDP (logged)		0.003***		−0.017		−0.009
		(0.001)		(0.012)		(0.019)
Population (logged)		0.008*		−0.0000		−0.020
		(0.004)		(0.051)		(0.047)
Year = 2010	−0.001	0.012***	0.030***	0.185***	0.033***	0.084**
	(0.001)	(0.004)	(0.006)	(0.039)	(0.008)	(0.040)
Year = 2020	−0.001*	0.024***	0.050***	0.346***	0.095***	0.190**
	(0.001)	(0.008)	(0.007)	(0.079)	(0.010)	(0.77)
N	320	249	320	249	320	249
Adjusted R-squared	0.756	0.777	.885	0.866	0.850	0.853

Notes: ***p<0.01, **p<0.05, and *p<0.1. Country-fixed effects are not shown.

Next, we wanted to test whether constitutional provisions interacted with measures of feminist mobilization. Since there are three constitutional provisions in each of the models, that would require three interaction terms; interpreting the marginal effects of any one of the constitutional provision variables would be difficult. As an alternative test, we subdivided the data according to the measure of feminist mobilization (scored 1, 2, and 3) and ran separate estimates to see whether egalitarian provisions had a greater effect in countries where feminist mobilization is high compared to countries where mobilization is low. If the marginal effects change across the three groups, there would be a strong case for including an interaction term. However, the marginal effects are similar across the subsets except for the customary law variable, which has higher marginal effects for the middle score on feminist mobilization (see Appendix Table 2).

Finally, an important variable not included in these models is culture. There is considerable empirical evidence demonstrating the effect of culture and attitudes about the role of women in society on the level of women's representation in national legislatures (Norris and Inglehart 2001; Inglehart and Norris 2003; Paxton and Kunovich 2003; Ruedin 2012). Paxton and Kunovich (2003), for example, found that cultural beliefs were the best predictor of women's political power. However, cultural attitudes are difficult to measure cross-nationally and over time. The commonly used World Values Survey (WVS) data are not available for several of our country cases; for the countries that are surveyed, there is only one survey data point, or if there are two survey data points, it is usually not for the same two time periods across countries. In short, using WVS data would reduce the number of observations by about half or more. Other measures we know of capture attitudes at only one point in time.

In the absence of time series data, we ran a cross-sectional regression including a culture variable using the 2015 data. We used the discriminatory norms component of the Women, Peace, and Security Index,[16] which shows the percentage of males aged 15 or older who agree it is unacceptable for women to work. The cross-sectional results are similar in terms of the sign of the coefficients, but egalitarian and maternal provisions are no longer statistically significant, while customary law becomes significant (results not shown). Since this is cross-sectional instead of panel data, we cannot include country-fixed effects; the panel regressions indicate that there is unmeasured heterogeneity. Thus, we determined that the panel data approach is better than cross-sectional regressions that include a variable for culture.

Conclusion

This chapter has presented data on gender provisions across countries and over time. Drawing upon our database of gender rights, we found that egalitarian rights are associated with stronger legal frameworks in issue areas that affect women's social and economic equality. In a more robust multivariate analysis, we found that egalitarian provisions are positively and significantly associated with higher scores on the Global Gender Gap Index and its subindices, while maternal provisions have a negative effect. These results are rather remarkable given that the countries that are most likely to adopt egalitarian provisions are mostly in the lower income category and/or are among the countries with a high degree of inequality between women and men (see again Table 3.1 and Figure 3.6). The positive impact of egalitarian provisions may become even more pronounced over time as institutional changes can sometimes take decades to take full effect (Keith et al. 2009; Wolbrecht and Corder 2020).

Any statistical analysis faces the challenge of linking constitutional provisions to a distant observable empirical outcome, such as the Gender Gap Index. After constitutional rights are established, there are many intervening steps before outcomes improve substantially: women must claim their rights, secure policy changes, and get states and courts to enforce these policies. To better understand how constitutional provisions matter on the ground, in terms of both process and mid-range legislative and judicial outcomes, the next two chapters provide qualitative case studies based on field research in Latin America and Southern Africa.

Chapter Appendix

APPENDIX TABLE 1 WEF Global Gender Gap Subindices by Region and Income Group, 2021

	Health and Survival	*Economic Participation and Opportunity*	*Political Empowerment*
Anglo countries	0.968	0.735	0.403
East Asia and the Pacific	0.969	0.686	0.136
Eastern Europe and Central Asia	0.976	0.694	0.162
Latin America and the Caribbean	0.974	0.663	0.281
The Middle East and North Africa	0.964	0.458	0.117
South Asia	0.957	0.433	0.215
Sub-Saharan Africa	0.973	0.690	0.218
Western and Southern Europe	0.969	0.730	0.400
High income	0.971	0.701	0.311
Upper middle income	0.971	0.640	0.223
Lower middle income	0.970	0.625	0.199
Low income	0.970	0.637	0.210
Mean	0.970	0.656	0.244
Standard deviation	0.009	0.126	0.157

APPENDIX TABLE 2 Regression results by level of feminist mobilization. Dependent variable = Global Gender Gap Index in 2020

	Level of Feminist Mobilization		
	1	*2*	*3*
Egalitarian	0.007	0.018	0.009
	(0.007)	(0.012)	(0.007)
Maternal	−0.017	−0.082	−0.004
	(0.012)	(0.054)	(0.007)
Customary law	−0.010	0.281*	−0.088
	(0.077)	(0.147)	(0.061)
Polity 2	0.0003	−0.008**	−0.003***
	(0.002)	(0.004)	(0.001)
Judicial independence	0.004	−0.003	−0.009
	(0.008)	(0.013)	(0.009)
Age of constitution	−0.005	−0.035	−0.001
	(0.009)	(0.031)	(0.001)
GDP (logged)	−0.003	−0.037	−0.007
	(0.011)	(0.030)	(0.021)
Population (logged)	0.022	0.005	0.081
	(0.037)	(0.092)	(0.076)
Year = 2010	0.068	−0.305	0.012
	(0.088)	(0.308)	(0.011)
Year = 2020	0.140	−0.619	0.037***
	(0.177)	(0.626)	(0.014)
N	102	77	66
Adjusted R-squared	0.898	0.838	0.944

Notes: ***p<0.01, **p<0.05, and *p<0.1.

Notes

1 The OECD Development Centre has been publishing the Social Institutions and Gender Index (SIGI) since 2009.

2 Ecuador's Constitution also includes provisions that prioritize victims of sexual and domestic violence for care in the private and public sector (Article 35), mandates special procedures for the prosecution of domestic violence and related crimes, and the appointment of specialized prosecutors and attorneys (Article 81), prohibits advertisements that foment violence or sexism (Article 19), and obligates the state to eliminate all forms of violence in the education system and "to safeguard the bodily, psychological and sexual integrity of students" (Article 347). And Article 393 states, "The State shall guarantee human safety by means of integrated policies and actions to ensure the peaceful coexistence of persons, to promote a culture of peace and to prevent forms of violence and discrimination and the perpetration of offenses and crimes. The planning and application of these policies shall be entrusted to specialized bodies at the different levels of government."

3 Two countries in our database have introduced abortion bans (with limited exceptions) in their national constitutions. These include Kenya (Article 26, sec. 4) and Somalia (Article 15, sec. 5).

4 The Gender Gap subindices that we use are measured as follows: economic participation and opportunity are based on the labor force participation rate, wage equality, estimated earned income, professional and technical workers, legislators, senior officials and managers; health and survival is measured by the sex ratio at birth and healthy life expectancy; and political empowerment is measured by women in parliament, women in ministerial positions, and years with a female head of state (last 50 years). WEF, "Global Gender Gap Report 2021."

5 The Historical Gender Equality Index (HGEI) captures many of the same differences in outcomes between men and women. However, it covers fewer countries (129) and ends in 2003. Since our analysis examines the effect of constitutional provisions on outcomes about five years later (and in some models, 10–15 years later), this measure would not allow us to test for longer term effects of constitutional provisions.

6 Similar to health and survival, the subindex measuring educational attainment also exhibits much less variation across countries. Separate statistics on educational empowerment are not shown.

7 Paulson-Smith and Tripp (2021) also document this major shift to include gender rights in African constitutions.

8 Another variable that is often included as an explanatory variable is the ratification of the CEDAW. All but seven countries in our database have ratified the CEDAW and 90% of our countries ratified CEDAW before or at the time our panel data begins. There would be little or no variation on this variable across countries or over time, so we did not include CEDAW ratification in our panel data analysis.

9 The international human rights law literature has done more to incorporate measures of civil society strength into quantitative analyses. See, for example, Hafner-Burton and Tsutsui (2005), Neumayer (2005), and Simmons (2009), who control for domestic strength and presence of international NGOs in their analyses of the effect of international treaties.

10 See, for example, Brinks and Botero (2014), Gelb (2003), McBride and Mazur (2010), and Tripp et al. (2008).

11 The FMI distinguishes between women's movements and feminist movements that seek to improve women's status. The FMI codes for the existence of a feminist movement, whether it is independent of the state, political parties, and other male-dominated organizations (autonomy), and its ability to influence media, political agendas, and discourse (strength). Additional information about the index and coding can be found at: www.sfu.ca/politics/feministmovement/data-maps.html.

12 Source: Polity IV Project, Political Regime Characteristics and Transitions, 1800–2018, Integrated Network for Societal Conflict Research (INSCR). Available at: www.systemicpeace.org/inscrdata.html.

13 Source: Cingranelli, David L., David L. Richards, and K. Chad Clay. 2014. "The CIRI Human Rights Dataset." Their index scores judicial independence as follows: 0 = not independent, 1 = partially independent, and 2 = generally independent. Available at: www.humanrightsdata.com.

14 GDP per capita and population statistics are from the World Bank's World Development Indicators. Available at: https://data.worldbank.org/indicator/NY.GDP.PCAP.CD.

15 The WEF Global Gender Gap data are from 2006 to 2021 with the data collapsed or averaged for three distinct periods. Constitutional provisions are measured in 1995, 2005, and 2015. Ideally, we would measure the dependent variable five years later for each panel. However, due to data limitations, the lags vary: for the 1995 provisions, the dependent variable is the average of 2006 and 2007 Gender Gap indices, the earliest WEF observations; for the 2005 provisions, the dependent variable is the average of the 2009, 2010, and 2011 indices; and for the 2015 provisions, the dependent variable is the average of 2018 (pre-covid) and 2021 indices.

16 The Women, Peace and Security Index is available at: https://giwps.georgetown.edu/the-index/chapters/.

References

Albertyn, Catherine. 2017. "Women and constitution-making in South Africa." In *Constitutions and Gender*, edited by Helen Irving, 47–80. Cheltenham: Edward Elgar Publishing.

Beer, Caroline. 2009. "Democracy and Gender Equality." *Studies in Comparative International Development* 44, no. 3: 212–227.

Blasi, Gerald J. and David Cingranelli. 1996. "Do Constitutions and Institutions Help Protect Human Rights?" *Human Rights and Developing Countries* 4: 223–237.

Brinks, Daniel and Sandra Botero. 2014. "Inequality and the Rule of Law: Ineffective Rights in Latin American Democracies." In *Reflections on Uneven Democracies: The Legacy of Guillermo O'Donnell*, edited by Daniel Brinks, Marcelo Leiras, and Scott Mainwaring, 214–239. Baltimore: Johns Hopkins University Press.

Crabtree, Charles and Michael J. Nelson. 2017. "New Evidence for a Positive Relationship Between De Facto Judicial Independence and State Respect for Empowerment Rights." *International Studies Quarterly* 61, no. 1: 210–224.

Chilton, Adam S. and Mila Versteeg. 2016. "Do Constitutional Rights Make a Difference?" *American Journal of Political Science* 60, no. 3: 575–589.

Chilton, Adam S. and Mila Versteeg. 2020. *How Constitutional Rights Matter*. New York: Oxford University Press.

Dobrowolsky, Alexandra and Vivien Hart. 2003. "Introduction: Women, New Politics and Constitutional Change." In *Women Making Constitutions: New Politics and Comparative Perspectives*, edited by Alexandra Dobrowolsky and Vivien Hart, 1–19. New York: Palgrave Macmillan.

Elkins, Zachary, Tom Ginsburg, and Beth Ann Simmons. 2013. "Getting to Rights: Treaty Ratification, Constitutional Convergence, and Human Rights Practice." *Harvard International Law Journal* 54, no. 1: 61–95.

Gelb, Joyce. 2003. *Gender Policies in Japan and the United States: Comparing Women's Movements, Rights and Politics*. New York: Palgrave Macmillan.

Hafner-Burton, Emilie and Kiyoteru Tsutsui. 2005. "Human Rights in a Globalizing World: The Paradox of Empty Promises." *American Journal of Sociology* 110, no. 5: 1373–1411.

Htun, Mala and Laurel S. Weldon. 2012. "The Civic Origins of Progressive Policy Change: Combating Violence Against Women in Global Perspective, 1975–2005." *American Political Science Review* 106, no. 3: 548–569.

Htun, Mala and S. Laurel Weldon. 2018. *The Logics of Gender Justice: State Action on Women's Rights around the World*. New York: Cambridge University Press.

Inglehart, Ronald and Pippa Norris. 2003. *Rising Tide*. New York: Cambridge University Press.

Irving, Helen. 2008. *Gender and the Constitution: Equity and Agency in Comparative Constitutional Design*. Cambridge: Cambridge University Press.

Keith, Linda Camp. 2002. "Constitutional Provisions for Individual Human Rights (1976–1996): Are They More Than Mere Window Dressing?" *Political Research Quarterly* 55: 111–143.

Keith, Linda Camp, C. Neal Tate, and Steven Poe. 2009. "Is the Law a Mere Parchment Barrier to Human Rights Abuse?" *The Journal of Politics* 71, no. 2: 644–660.

Law, David and Mila Versteeg. 2011. "The Evolution and Ideology of Global Constitutionalism." *California Law Review* 99: 1163–1254.

Law, David and Mila Versteeg. 2013. "Sham Constitutions." *California Law Review* 101, no. 4: 863–952.

McBride, Dorothy E. and Amy G. Mazur. 2010. *The Politics of State Feminism*. Philadelphia: Temple University Press.

Metelska-Szaniawska, Katarzyna and Jacek Lewkowicz. 2021. "Post-socialist "Illiberal Democracies:" Do de jure Constitutional Rights Matter?" *Constitutional Political Economy* 32, no. 2: 233–265.

Melton, James. 2014. "Do Constitutional Rights Matter?" unpublished paper. Available at: https://pdfs.semanticscholar.org/e030/faaef3401760e608dfb9faa13389bd41d377.pdf.

Neumayer, Eric. 2005. "Do International Human Rights Treaties Improve Respect for Human Rights?" *Journal of Conflict Resolution* 49, no. 6: 925–953.

Norris, Pippa and Ronald Inglehart. 2001. "Cultural Obstacles to Equal Representation." *Journal of Democracy* 12, no. 3: 126–140.

Pamela Paxton and Sheri Kunovich. 2003. "Women's Political Representation: The Importance of Ideology." *Social Forces* 82, no. 1: 87–114.

Paulson-Smith, Kaden and Aili Mari Tripp. 2021. "Women's Rights and Critical Junctures in Constitutional Reform in Africa (1951–2019)." *African Affairs* 120, no. 480: 365–389.

Ruedin, Dieder. 2012. "The Representation of Women in National Parliaments: A Cross-national Comparison." *European Sociological Review* 28, no. 1: 96–109.

Simmons, Beth. 2009. *Mobilizing for Human Rights: International Law in Domestic Politics*. Cambridge: Cambridge University Press.

Suk, Julie. 2018. "Gender Equality and the Protection of Motherhood in Global Constitutionalism." *Law & Ethics of Human Rights* 12, no. 1: 151–180.

Tripp, Aili Mari, Isabel Casimiro, Joy Kwesiga, and Alice Mungwa. 2008. *African Women's Movements: Transforming Political Landscapes*. New York: Cambridge University Press.

Tsutsui, Kiyoteru, Claire Whitlinger, and Alwyn Lim. 2012. "International Human Rights Law and Social Movements: States' Resistance and Civil Society's Insistence." *Annual Review of Law and Social Science* 8: 367–396.

Weldon, Laurel S. 2002. *Protest, Policy, and the Problem of Violence Against Women: A Cross-National Comparison*. Pittsburgh, PA: University of Pittsburgh Press.

Wolbrecht, Christina, and J. Kevin Corder. 2020. "Turning Rights Into Ballots: The Uneven Integration of Women Into Electoral Politics after Suffrage." *PS, Political Science & Politics* 53, no.3: 479–483.

World Economic Forum (WEF). 2021. "Global Gender Gap Report 2021." *World Economic Forum*. Available at: https://www.weforum.org/reports/global-gender-gap-report-2021/in-full

4

GENDER PROVISIONS, RIGHTS ADVOCACY, AND POLICY OUTCOMES IN CHILE AND ARGENTINA

Priscilla A. Lambert and Druscilla L. Scribner

> The Constitution can be said to be neutral, but it is a neutrality of patriarchy, neutrality that does not name; a neutrality that is consumed [used] as male.
>
> —*Ministry of Labor, Chile, Interview*

> After [CEDAW was incorporated into the Constitution], there has been a redefinition of the constitutional standards in the practice of law. Legislative discourse, in Congress, in standards, in administrative decisions, has been transformed. Numerous [pieces of legislation] capture the development and evolution of international human rights law, now part of Argentine constitutional law, in the justification of laws, in parliamentary debates, and in the justifications for administrative decisions.
>
> —*Legal Scholar, Argentina, Interview*

Introduction

In the hands of women's rights advocates, gender equality provisions have the potential to provide a legal basis for work to advance new policy, protect policy gains, and pursue rights-based litigation. Argentina and Chile share more than 5,000 miles of border and many historical, political, and social experiences, but their constitutions differ in how they recognize gender equality. The Argentine Constitution contains several specific provisions that recognize and seek to advance gender equality. It also acknowledges and incorporates international law: several international human rights treaties have constitutional status in Argentina. The Chilean Constitution was amended in 1999 to contain a sex equality statement; however, it does not actively redress gender

DOI: 10.4324/9781003303725-4

discrimination. This chapter draws on legislation, legislative debates, high court cases, and interviews with women's rights advocates to show that in Chile, where egalitarian provisions are minimal, activists face more limitations than Argentinian activists in their efforts to pursue policies that contribute to women's equality.[1]

Argentina and Chile are similar in several important ways. They are among the most economically developed Latin American countries. Each is predominantly Catholic, and the Church is a critical non-state political actor in issues affecting the family, especially reproductive health policies. Catholicism also has an important influence on the culture of both countries. In Chile and Argentina, cultural attitudes about gender roles are often a barrier to the legislation and implementation of policies that promote women's equality. Both countries experienced a prolonged period of repressive military rule in the 1970s and 1980s (Chile from 1973 to 1990 and Argentina from 1976 to 1983), followed by re-democratization and neo-liberal economic restructuring. Strong women's movements emerged in both countries and played a significant role in bringing down authoritarian regimes (Jaquette 2001; Waylen 2007, 66). Today, women's rights organizations are professionalized and well-connected to international networks of women's and human rights groups.[2] Both countries are exposed to global and regional pressures to implement policies and strengthen national gender machinery to improve women's lives (Craske and Molyneux 2002, 10–11). Finally, the women's movement experienced fragmentation in both countries after the democratic transition (Alvarez, Dagnino, and Escobar 1998, 306–308; Vargas 2002).

The two countries also have significant differences. Argentina is a federal system, which notably complicates policy implementation. Moreover, Argentina is a regional leader in adopting a gender quota, and there are proportionally more women in parliament in Argentina than in Chile. However, the degree to which this presence of women translates into substantive representation is debated (Franceschet and Piscopo 2008).[3] Left parties, which are more likely (but not guaranteed) to promote women's equality, have been fragmented in Argentina. This tempers the potential impact of the gender quota and left parties on gender policy. With regard to the gender machinery, Chile's National Office of Women's Affairs or SERNAM (Servicio Nacional de la Mujer)[4] has been an important ally in achieving policy change and generally has been more influential than its Argentine counterpart, the National Women's Council (CNM, Consejo Nacional de la Mujer) (Franceschet 2008, 2010; Ríos Tobar 2009). Interviewees in government agencies and the legislature in Argentina said the CNM was institutionally weak and suffered from a lack of "budget, hierarchy and legitimacy." On the other hand, at times, SERNAM's ties to the conservative Christian Democratic Party and the political role of the Church have dampened the scope of reform efforts in Chile (Blofield and Haas 2005; Ríos Tobar 2007).

Constitutional Provisions and Policy Change—Expectations

As noted earlier, if constitutional provisions are to be effective, they must be taken up, claimed, and used by political and social actors. Following the theoretical arguments outlined in Chapter 2, we expect gender provisions to affect processes and outcomes in the legislative and judicial arenas: To help legitimize rights-based discourse, enable policy reform in the legislature, and provide legal tools and arguments that shape legal claims and their adjudication in courts.

Enhances the Legitimacy of Rights Claims

Constitutional rights and duties reflect shared national values and identity. A constitutional commitment to gender equality should increase the legitimacy of gender rights and ground arguments for gender policy change. For both countries, we examine the congressional record to assess how constitutional provisions shape the process, such as the language and discourse when legislators introduce, frame, and debate gender policy. Women's rights arguments and proposals should be more common in Argentina, where constitutional values about gender equality are explicit and thus provide more constitutional legitimacy than is available in Chile. We expect to see greater reliance on international law arguments in Chile because its constitution does not provide a strong legal platform for gender equality.

Enables Policy Change

As described in Chapter 2, constitutional provisions can be part of an enabling framework that facilitates policy change. In Argentina, egalitarian constitutional provisions provide a foundation for women's rights claims; accordingly, we expect policymakers and women's rights advocates to identify egalitarian constitutional provisions as a central tool to pursue policy change. We also expect different policy outcomes and generally more gender policy in Argentina. Likewise, we expect legislative discourse and legislation to draw on egalitarian language in the constitution. In the Chilean case, we expect the absence of egalitarian provisions to hinder advocates. Because Chile amended the Constitution to include a sex equality statement in 1999, we can also examine how advocates see this constitutional change as helpful for achieving policy change.

Provides Legal Tools and Arguments

Constitutional rights similarly create tools for litigation that may affect the judicial interpretation of laws and the protection and advancement of constitutional rights. Constitutional provisions create or limit opportunities for rights-based litigation and affect the persuasiveness of rights-based arguments. If gender equality provisions in the national constitution improve the opportunity to advance litigation on women's rights and/or improve the chances of "women-friendly" decisions, we would expect to see more substantial litigation efforts and a greater probability of successful outcomes in Argentina.

Comparing Constitutions

We conducted 28 in-depth interviews (14 in each country) with several types of individuals: Leaders of non-governmental organizations and prominent women's movement activists, legislators, scholars, and researchers working on women's issues and gender justice, and former and current government officials in ministries involved in gender policy.

In the first part of this case study, we review the constitutional provisions and explain how interviewees view the constitution as informing their work and providing greater legitimacy for women's rights claims. In the second half of the analysis, we consider gender provisions and policy outcomes in three areas: gender-based violence, sexual and reproductive health, and employment rights. We examine the discourse, content, and framing of gender policy bills, committee and floor debates, and the text of the law. In each policy area, we trace key pieces of legislation from the bill stage through the passage, analyzing legislative floor debates as well as the final law. In our interviews with individuals (some of whom were closely involved with specific pieces of legislation), we solicited their informed opinion about the scope of each policy and its passage. Concerning litigation, we examined the record of high court decisions during the same timeframe. We also discussed litigation strategies and individual cases with our interviewees, asking whether and how gender provisions were reflected in judicial decisions.

Part I: Gender in the Constitution

Argentina

The Argentine Constitution dates to 1853. Significant constitutional reform was enacted in 1994 and included several changes with respect to gender. The changes incorporated three key provisions promoting gender equality: a constitutional electoral quota (Article 37), an equal pay for equal work provision (Article 14 bis), and an affirmative action provision that gives Congress the power to "legislate and promote positive measures guaranteeing true equality of opportunity and treatment" (Article 75, No. 23). According to one lawyer, these provisions were adopted with "a clear political intention to overcome obstacles in the road to equality [and provide the legal] tools and argumentation to overcome existing inequalities. Affirmative action is a very important point in this regard . . . It has had a transformative effect."[5] It has also served as an important defense against claims that affirmative action violates the right to equality before the law (Lubertino 2003).

In addition, and perhaps most importantly, Argentina's 1994 Constitution explicitly names and incorporates core provisions of the UN Convention on the Elimination of All Forms of Discrimination against Women, CEDAW (Article 75, No. 22).[6] As one lawyer explained, "the incorporation of the CEDAW convention to the Constitution . . . has transformed our understanding and reading of all rights; it was, and is, central to understanding women's rights in the Constitution."[7] Others described it as a crucial advance for women because it provides the legal tools for getting women's issues on the legislative agenda, plays a key role in lobbying and efforts to promote legislative change, and opens the "way for women and women's organizations to use the courts to gain the enforcement of women's rights nationally" (Kohen 2009, 95).[8] One legal scholar and activist noted that the inclusion of CEDAW in the Constitution had resulted in a major cultural shift in the legislature and the legislative process:

> Legislative discourse, in Congress . . . has been transformed. Numerous [pieces of legislation] capture the development and evolution of international law of human rights, now part of Argentine constitutional law, in the justification of laws, in parliamentary debates, and in the justifications for administrative decisions.[9]

International treaties such as CEDAW can be used to legitimize rights-based claims and remind Argentine legislators and judges that they are subject to these laws. For the issue of violence against women, constitutional and international law made a difference through the "diffusion of standards, the circulation of reports, and the jurisprudence of concrete cases. I think it has advanced the national discussion."[10] Although the ordinary judiciary's use and awareness of international law are much less common, superior courts are more likely to reference international law, comparative law, and regional decisions (by the Inter-American Commission and Inter-American Court of Human Rights):

> Now when the judiciary has to take up a gender-specific case, judges and lawyers have much more information to argue for the rights of women, and a lot more awareness about what is acceptable, and about what kind of discrimination is not permissible than 20 years ago.[11]

Scholars, activists, and legislators consistently described the 1994 Constitution as "promoting equality," as central to their activities, and "definitely a tool" to redress past discrimination through public policy and litigation.[12] Advocates also agreed that their efforts were aided or enabled by the Constitution; they used constitutional provisions as a pedagogical tool to instruct judges, legislators, and the public about the Constitution and to remind them that the government is obligated to act.[13] Many cited instances where egalitarian provisions helped further particular efforts in the legislative and judicial arenas.[14]

Several interviewees referred to constitutional provisions increasing the legitimacy of rights claims and helping bring about change in cultural attitudes. In the words of one women's rights lawyer in Argentina:

> [The Constitution] definitely helps. It gives legitimacy to arguments and proposals that would otherwise be very arduous to make. There are still several areas where stereotypes are deeply rooted, and constitutionally based arguments can be a source for movement and change, a way to push the limits in conservative provinces.[15]

At the same time, our interviewees, particularly those working in or with the state, viewed the implementation of law as problematic. The difficulties stem from several factors, including low administrative capacity and federalism, lack of funding, lack of accountability, the absence of a sense of responsibility on the part of the state to ensure that individual rights are taken into account when accessing state services, and continued gender stereotyping within state agencies (particularly the judiciary). Women's organizations reported that they divide their efforts between holding the state accountable for implementing the policy that has already been passed and advocating for additional policies. In both cases, constitutional provisions aid their efforts.

Chile

Chile transitioned to democracy with the 1980 "Constitution in Liberty," a document written by the military regime and "inspired by right-wing philosopher Friedrich Hayek" (Waylen 2007, 158). Given its roots in the military dictatorship (1973–1989), those on the political left have long contested the Constitution's legitimacy (more on this later). Article 1 of the Constitution contains a neutral statement of equality (using the neutral term "all persons"); it also singles out the family as the fundamental unit of society and obligates the state to take steps to protect and strengthen the family. In 1999, the Constitution was amended to explicitly include a statement that men and women are equal before the law (Law 19,611, now part of Article 19, No. 2). The Chilean Constitution, however, does not promote gender equality or address gender discrimination, nor does it actively promote or protect motherhood.[16] Thus, we classify the Chilean Constitution as mostly neutral toward gender (Lambert and Scribner 2009). Interviewees universally confirmed this view of the Constitution, though many argued that neutrality masked and perpetuated patriarchy: "the text is neutral, [but] the debate and thinking behind it was not."[17]

The gender-neutral Constitution appears to be marginal to the activities of women's rights advocates, while provisions on the family often have a negative impact. When asked about how constitutional provisions and values shape policy, many interviewees felt the Constitution was not a tool or even "the main obstacle to achieving progress."[18] Most believed that the equality statement was symbolically important, but the provision on family carried far more weight: "the [constitutional provision] that is most commonly used is the recognition of the family as the fundamental unit of society."[19] Many suggested that the political right had been more active and adept at using the Constitution to block gender policy than the political center or the left had been at achieving policy change.[20] Gender policy proposals face a stiff bargaining environment in Chile due to coalition politics. According to interviewees in both governmental and non-governmental positions, this often means that a discourse of women's rights and gender equality is strategically dropped for the more palatable and legislatively successful discourse of family and motherhood. As one legislator put it, "A discourse based on family, women as mothers, in the end, has much more weight and support than a discourse of women's rights."[21]

At the same time, recognizing equality under the law is not without significance. The 1999 amendment has served as a basis for revising or challenging discriminatory laws and achieving key policy advances. Interviewees working in government, civil society, and the legislature agreed that the equality statement had impacted the language of law and provided a formal basis of legitimacy of new laws. One legislator went so far as to say that without the constitutional equality provision, it would have been much harder to get some bills passed, particularly the equal pay law. Others suggested that the amendment had served as a starting point for negotiation, as an agreed-upon principle that helped to move the debate forward.[22]

Absent more concrete rights in the Constitution, many NGO activists and state actors have relied upon international law, particularly CEDAW and Belem do Para, to ground their legal arguments and to provide leverage for policy change in areas where the state was not meeting its international obligations. As one Chilean activist explained:

> International law is what we have used most often, along with other NGOs nationally and regionally. We have worked with CEDAW since the beginning and CEDAW has been the instrument to which we have turned for campaigns, diffusion of ideas and information.[23]

International law, however, is not a substitute for constitutional provisions. Although Article 5 recognizes the constitutional status of international treaties that are ratified and in force, the legal hierarchy of international law is debated and uncertain (Vicuña and Bauzá 2005).[24] Moreover, international law arguments may not find a ready audience among politicians who are less supportive of international law argumentation on sovereignty grounds or among judges who have been reluctant to apply human rights standards domestically. There is "general recognition among congressional members that international law is important and should be reflected in national legislation." But there is also a lack of awareness of international women's rights and obligations: "When it comes to actually passing a law . . . you run into cultural and ideological differences. There is a lot of resistance on sovereignty grounds, and because of the abortion issue with CEDAW."[25]

Those involved in human rights litigation echoed the view that the Constitution was "not particularly helpful" for pursuing gender policy reform. Litigators explained that "very few women are using the courts to press inequality claims," though this is due in part to a legal culture that prefers arguments (and judgments) based on statute rather than using the Constitution as the "starting point for legal argument and interpretation."[26] Similarly, a UN working group observed that "the courts do not provide a realistic recourse for women on issues of equality," nor are they "known for demonstrating gender sensitivity."[27] In short, "Women have not used the . . . judicial tools to protect the principle of equality or to protect or amplify their rights."[28] In recent years, scholars have seen a gender perspective in judicial reasoning beginning to develop.[29] Some "incipient activism in rights adjudication in Chile" may result from judicial training and institutional changes. However, in the early 2000s, there was no clear trend toward a "rights revolution" (Couso and Hilbink 2011, 100–112).

Recognizing the limitations of the current Constitution, activists have devoted considerable energy to reforming it. As part of his "Women's Agenda," President Sebastian Piñera proposed to revise Article 1 of the Constitution to include the following statement: "It is also the duty of the State to promote equality of rights and dignity between women and men, avoiding all forms of violence, abuse or arbitrary discrimination."[30] In the first floor discussion of the bill, those supporting the reform noted the importance of constitutional recognition and state promotion of gender equality and the impact it would have on future legislation and jurisprudence. For example, Congresswoman Carmen Hertz stated that approval of the reform will "give a legal imperative to the state's power, its 'duty' to 'respect' and 'promote' equality [between men and women] that goes beyond equality before the law." Similarly, Congresswoman Loreto Carvajal argued that constitutional reform would create a new baseline and "condition all aspects of our legislative work in areas such as education, health, social, economic, wage, work and, of course, protection." Congressman Osvaldo Urrutia added that the reform "opens the possibility of standardized jurisprudence to establish or ratify that men and women are equal before the law."[31] These comments mirror our main theoretical expectations: that constitutional provisions matter for the legitimacy of rights claims, as an enabling framework for legislation, and as a legal anchor for judicial decisions.

Significant constitutional changes may be on the horizon. In October 2020, Chileans went to the polls and overwhelmingly voted in favor of writing a new constitution. A constitutional convention with equal numbers of women and men was elected in April 2021. The draft produced included gender egalitarian provisions and many other rights for under-represented groups. Although this draft was rejected in a national vote on September 4, 2022, the strong support for a new constitution means that efforts to rewrite the Constitution will not end here. We return to this reform process in the concluding chapter.

Part II: Gender Policy

This section compares legislative reforms and judicial decisions in three key gender policy areas: Gender-based violence, sexual and reproductive health, and employment rights. We pay particular attention to laws that address common issues or appear similar in content in both countries. In Argentina, legislation, policy debates, and reforms often reflect the constitutional commitment to gender equality and are more likely to obligate the state to act and fulfill constitutional guarantees. In Chile, legislative debates reflect competing frames of reference, one stressing gender-neutral equality and the other stressing family protection. Gender-specific bills emphasizing women's role within the family (rather than gender equality) have a better chance of passing.

With respect to litigation, the picture is mixed and partial in both countries. The judiciary is a conservative institution and has not been a major player in defining gender rights. In both countries, the law and the courts are not seen as favorable venues for advocacy by women's rights organizations. Interviewees suggested that gender equality arguments have not been a winning strategy for litigators. Another significant hurdle for legal mobilization is that few lawyers and judges have the capacity to take on women's rights arguments or an interest in doing so (Ruibal 2015). While few gender equality cases are litigated in either country, in Chile the number of cases is especially small and gender equality claims are even rarer. The Argentine courts have been more active, increasingly incorporating international law and treaties (which, again, have constitutional status) that obligate judges to take women's rights more seriously.[32] This strategy has produced some landmark decisions.

Gender-Based Violence

Gender-based violence is arguably the most serious threat confronting women in any country. Chile and Argentina are no exception. Neither the Chilean nor the Argentine Constitution includes specific provisions about gender-based violence. However, both ratified the Inter-American Convention on the Prevention, Punishment, and Eradication of Violence against Women (commonly known as the Convention Belém do Pará) in 1996, and both are obligated to introduce measures to eliminate or limit violence against women and to monitor it. In Argentina, Belém do Pará and CEDAW have constitutional status. Argentina's Violence Against Women law explicitly draws upon constitutional rights, the principle of gender equality, and international law. In Chile, the framing of legislative debates and the law itself focus on the family and women's role within it.

Argentina

In Argentina, the 1994 Protection from Family Violence Law "constituted a major victory for the feminist movement, which had campaigned for this legal tool for years" (Kohen 2009, 87). Nonetheless, it suffered from numerous weaknesses: it was not consistently enforced; it was not considered part of criminal law; and it failed to take a comprehensive view of the causes of violence against women. The Law for the Comprehensive Protection of Women (No. 26.485), passed in 2009, represented a major legal advance. In particular, it draws on the constitutional right to equality between men and women and the international agreements referenced in Article 75 of the Constitution: CEDAW, the Convention Belém do Pará, and the Convention on the Rights of the Child. The law incorporates the broad definition of violence of the Convention Belém do Pará, requires all levels of government to adopt the means necessary to implement the law, mandates budgetary outlays, requires reporting and statistics generation, and obligates the state to act. The language of rights and gender equality permeates both the text of the 2009 statute and the legislative floor debates. For example, Representative Juliana Tullio declared, "finally we will have a standard to protect women's rights, sanction violence, and promote the right of women to live free from violence." Representative Silvia Storni emphasized that "advancing and attaining equality between women and men is a question of human rights."[33] However, the law's implementation has been hampered by Argentina's federal system and a weak CNM, which is in charge of oversight and implementation (Franceschet 2010; Smulovitz 2010).

Two other important laws have increased punishments for violent crimes against women. In 2012, Argentina revised the penal code to include femicide and made homicide for gender-related reasons an offense punishable by prison for life.[34] Large public protests against femicide and violence against women took place in 2015 and 2016 under the slogan and hashtag NiUnaMenos ("NotOneLess") and helped raise awareness and push for legal reforms.[35] The Rights and Guarantees of Crime Victims (No. 27.372/2017) goes further than the 2012 reform: It recognizes and guarantees the rights of victims and empowers authorities to prevent, investigate, and punish crimes, including crimes against sexual integrity and gender violence. It draws on the Constitutional recognition of international law and its first objective is to "guarantee the rights of victims of crimes and violations of human rights . . . as enshrined in the Argentine Constitution and international treaties of human rights that Argentina has ratified" (Law No. 27.372, Article 3a).

When individuals and advocates have turned to the courts in Argentina, they have run up against entrenched conservatism and gender bias. Judges may fail to investigate, dismiss cases of violence against women as a "private matter," require the victim to provide additional proof, and "re-victimize" the victim by focusing the investigation on a woman's body or character (Asensio 2010). A prominent example is L.N.P. v. Argentina (2007). L.N.P., a 15-year-old indigenous girl, was raped in a northern province by three men. Her injuries were extensive and verified, yet the judge doubted her lack of consent, suggesting that she did not resist seriously enough, that rape can be confused with violence common to the sexual act, and that the injuries were due to the nature of the act (anal penetration) and the youth of the subject. The UN Human Rights Committee found that the state violated the International Covenant on Civil and Political Rights. The case, which was followed in the national and local media, exemplifies the clash between a conservative judiciary and legislation that incorporates international definitions and standards of women's human rights (ELA 2009, 514).

Few gender-based violence cases make it to Argentina's Supreme Court. Most are heard in family courts or civil courts and then may be appealed to an appellate court. The decisions at these levels are mixed. As seen in L.N.P., some are highly discriminatory. However, a shift is occurring. Increasingly, the judiciary is actively drawing on constitutional rights and international law, changing its sentencing, "gradually modifying its practices to adapt to the requirements of international regulatory frameworks," and finding in favor of the victim (ELA 2011, 77).[36] Interviewees confirmed this trend and said that the responsibility of judges to investigate was being taken seriously at the appeals court level.[37] Higher courts, in particular, reflect these changes, at times drawing on constitutional and international law in their reasoning in gender-based violence cases.[38]

Chile

Chile does not have a comprehensive law to prevent violence against women. Congress passed anti-violence legislation in the mid-1990s and subsequently reformed the law in the 2000s. Although the original bill focused on gender and constitutional rights to life and equality before the law, the Family Violence Law (1994) faced a conservative political environment (over-representation of the right and a central role played by the Christian Democrats in the ruling coalition). The final bill was more moderate than activists wanted and was hamstrung by an inadequate budget, deficient judicial procedures, and weak penalties for perpetrators (Franceschet 2008).

A review of the floor debates over modifications to the 1994 family violence law demonstrates the rhetorical power of the constitutional provision regarding family, which is cited more frequently than arguments based on women's or human rights.[39] For example, Representative María Angélica Cristi's remarks clearly echo the constitutional provision on family: "We must recognize that the family is the fundamental unit in which humans socialize. A weak or unprotected family is at risk for violence." Other legislators, including members of the progressive Socialist Party, couched their support in similar terms. The final statute identifies inequality of power as a foundation for familial violence but does not identify gender inequality or acknowledge the gendered nature of family violence. The improvements to the 2005 law include increased penalties, the addition of physical and psychological violence to the criminal code, an overhaul of the family tribunals, an increased budget for shelters and data collection, and the creation and maintenance of national data registries to track the incidence and handling of domestic violence cases. Following this law's enactment, arrests for domestic violence more than doubled (Franceschet 2008). Despite these improvements, interviewees working in this area remained critical of the Family Violence Law. They noted that Chilean law continues to be limited to family violence and centers on a discourse of domestic violence rather than on the broader human rights discourse of gender-based violence that informs the Convention of Belém do Pará.[40]

The judiciary, and the criminal justice system in general, have not taken violence against women seriously. Evidence of this neglect can be seen in the low number of convictions and the status of the institutions themselves. The UNHCR reported in 2014 that although one in three Chilean women reported intimate partner violence, only 30% of women victims filed complaints, and only 8.8% of those complaints resulted in convictions.[41] The institutions that deal with violence against women also suffer from low status: "family courts and the inter-family violence judicial processes have a low value in the judiciary. No one wants to work there."[42] Gender stereotyping continues to be an issue in the judiciary, particularly at the lower court levels. This problem is exemplified in a 2016 "crime of passion" defense for attempted femicide.[43] When police officers responded, the woman's partner was brutally beating and stabbing her in their home and did not desist from the attack until one of the officers shot him. The partner was convicted of attempted femicide, but the trial court reduced the sentence to probation because the partner acted in a "fit of rage" over the victim's alleged infidelity.[44]

As noted earlier, few cases make it to the high courts, and litigation based on equality claims is rarely a winning strategy. Activists who do litigate violence against women cases rely heavily on international law, particularly CEDAW and Belém do Pará, to ground their legal arguments and pursue policy change in areas where the state is not meeting its international obligations.[45] According to one activist:

> International law is used frequently by the women's movement and women in government. And it has been [used] effectively, in the Violence Against

> Women law for example, . . . It is the tool we use most often in discourse, in political argumentation, in projects.[46]

But others contended that the equality clause has also been important and that it has been used "by the courts in their decisions and to support subsequent reforms. . . . Moreover, the criminal courts, in cases of violence against women, have applied this article."[47]

Workplace Equality

Recognizing and promoting gender equality and equal opportunities in the workplace, including via equal pay legislation, has been on the reform agenda for women's organizations in both countries during the three decades we study. Rights advocates pursuing workplace equality have drawn on the constitution and international commitments, but with different degrees of success and different discourses concerning equality.

Argentina

The Argentine Constitution (Section 14) includes the principle of equal pay for equal work and incorporates international law and treaties (Section 75) containing human rights principles regarding gender discrimination.[48] Additionally, the Constitution authorizes Congress to pass laws with positive (affirmative) actions to create a level playing field for women.

The Law on Employment Contracts (1976) regulates employment policy, including employment leave, wages, retirement regulations, as well as protections for female workers and maternity leave. After the transition to democracy, several pieces of legislation were passed that modify the Law on Employment Contracts in an egalitarian way. These changes were recognized in the National Plan for Equal Opportunity in the Workplace (1998). The National Plan lists the previous laws and international treaties ratified by Argentina that advance gender equality. These include equal opportunities and treatment for workers with family responsibilities, the right of all workers to upgrade their skills without discrimination, the right to equal pay for work of equal value, and protection from discrimination and sexual harassment in the workplace. The National Plan draws heavily on a discourse of gender equality in the Constitution, repeatedly notes the constitutional status of CEDAW in Argentina, and calls on the CNM to coordinate and implement these laws.

Subsequent employment laws often draw on constitutional rights and international treaties such as CEDAW provisions and ILO conventions in the text of the law and in legislative debates. For example, the 2002 Trade Union Quota Act, which established a 30% gender quota for trade union elections, explains in the preamble that the Constitution provides for legislation to promote equal opportunity and that the law "aims to give effect to this guarantee, so that women workers are represented in the discussion of their work conditions." Similarly, in legislative debates, senators referred to constitutional rights, equality of opportunity, and rights enshrined in ILO treaties that Argentina ratified.[49]

One of the most significant pieces of legislation affecting women's employment is the Domestic Worker Law (Law 26,844, 2013). This law granted domestic workers numerous rights and protections that regular workers enjoy under the Labor Contract Law, including maternity leave, paid holidays, yearly bonuses, compensation for dismissal, social security contributions, and limits on working hours. A unique feature of this law, and one that is important for ensuring the representation of domestic workers, is that it establishes the National Commission of Household Staff—a tripartite commission with union and government representatives charged with regulating minimum wage and working conditions for domestic workers (Gorban and Tizziani 2018). The law closely follows the principles and recommendations laid out in the ILO's Decent Work for Domestic Workers Convention No. 189 and Recommendation No. 201, which Argentina ratified in the same year.[50] The incorporation of international treaties in the Constitution, along with mobilization by international and domestic workers' unions, helped get this law on the agenda (Poblete 2018). As one Ministry of Labor official explained:

> The reform of the Constitution, the incorporation of international treaties, has affected the topics of legislation and the advances we have made. Last year the ILO worked on the issue of domestic workers, and this year too; this has generated political agendas and discussions about the topic. It has led to mobilization.[51]

In legislative debates, representatives and senators framed their arguments in terms of equality among workers, arguing that the disconnect between domestic workers' rights and those of other workers went against constitutional norms, and/or referred to their obligations to meet the standards of the ILO Convention. For example, Representative Juan Mario Pais argued, "Today is an historic day . . . because we are legislating for inclusion and eliminating discrimination that was an affront to the National Constitution. Obviously, we are beginning to work fully in pursuit of the protection imposed by Article 14 bis of our Basic Law."[52]

Court decisions on employment policy reflect, to some extent, the egalitarian Constitution. *Asociación Mujeres en Igualdad v. Freddo S.A* (16 December 2002) is a landmark sex discrimination case involving discriminatory hiring practices. The judge cited the constitutional right to "real equality of opportunities" (Article 75) and international commitments in his decision and imposed fines and affirmative action measures on Freddo to correct the discrimination. This was the first case in which the Argentine judicial branch imposed this remedy. In *Mirtha Graciela and others v. Taldelva SRL and others/amparo* (May 20, 2014), a woman in Salta

Province who met all the requirements to be hired as a bus driver claimed she was not given a job because she was a woman. Since no women had ever been hired by the bus company, the provincial court judge ruled that no other proof of discrimination was needed. Her suit made important rights-based arguments about gender equality, discrimination on the basis of gender, and the violation of women's rights. The judge imposed a quota (30%) for female driver positions, a decision that was vacated on appeal by Salta's Superior Tribunal. However, the national Supreme Court sided with the provincial court on appeal. It based its decision on constitutional rights to equality, non-discrimination, and constitutional international human rights commitments, including CEDAW obligations. These two decisions are significant because they impose affirmative action remedies on private-sector businesses. Instead of obligating the state to act, the court obligated private actors to take proactive measures.

Chile

Changes in Chilean labor law reflect a tension between the constitutional commitments to family and to equality before the law. Some important legislation advancing women's rights in the workplace has been passed, such as the Sexual Harassment Law and the Equal Pay Law. At the same time, even policy changes potentially supportive of gender equality in the workplace are often framed in terms of women's traditional caregiving role and constitutional protection of the family.[53]

The 2002 Child Care Act is a good example. This law that required businesses to establish on-site nurseries for their female employees was supposed to enable more mothers to remain in the workforce and was described as "an important support for motherhood." In reality, it "implicitly accepts childcare as solely a woman's responsibility" (Blofield and Haas 2005, 54). A 2009 bill proposed to extend this right to fathers when the mother was absent or unable to care for a child under two; however, the law in its final form applies only to widowed fathers or fathers with sole custody. The legislation of paternity leave also focused on the family and Article 1 of the Constitution, which states that the family is the fundamental nucleus of society. Legislators argued that because motherhood is necessary for that nucleus, it follows that fathers should have leave at the birth of a child to "support the mother and child precisely in the moment in which they need additional care and contribute to stronger bonds of affection within the nuclear family."[54]

Tracing the passage of the Act on Sexual Harassment in the Workplace reveals a similar pattern. In justifying the amendments to the labor code to make sexual harassment illegal and set up a complaint mechanism, SERNAM and the main sponsor, Representative Adriana Muñoz, made direct reference to women's rights: "If the bill is passed in Congress, it will . . . send a powerful signal that more women and young women can enter the employment world confident in the knowledge that their rights will be respected."[55] However, by 2005, when the final version of the bill came to a vote, there was no mention of women's rights or constitutional rights. In her final defense of the law, Adriana Muñoz herself did not refer to rights or even dignity but returned to the theme of family: "Considering the proportion of female-headed households with dependent children, the fact that their jobs are constantly in question because of abuse of power makes their situation all the more dramatic."[56] Moreover, cases of sexual harassment have not fared particularly well in the courts because of the need to prove significant harassment to judges in a context where sexual harassment has become naturalized and accepted.[57]

The Equal Pay Law (2009) is clearly aimed at advancing equality and is based on gender equality arguments. This law represents a departure from the previous emphasis on women's role in the family by explicitly tying the legislation to gender equality and non-discrimination provisions in the Constitution as well as international law and practice.[58] Some interviewees went so far as to say that the constitutional equality provision was key to passing this law.[59] On the occasion of its passage, President Bachelet declared that Chile was now "fulfilling an ethical obligation to demonstrate that men and women are equal before the law" (Irarrázaval and Massuh 2014, 254). Its proponents, however, hastened to add that it was not just women's rights that were at stake, but also family stability, since women contribute significantly to family income: "Wage discrimination, not only undermines the rights of women . . . [it] is contrary to the interests, and even the stability of the family."[60] Finally, despite being more egalitarian than many other laws passed in this period, the Equal Pay Law nonetheless suffers from several weaknesses and significant legal loopholes that allow employers to continue paying male workers more.[61]

Finally, Chile, like Argentina, passed reforms to improve the status of domestic workers; these changes came about as a result of mobilization by domestic workers' associations and the ILO's Convention No. 189. The ratifications of C189 and the domestic worker bill were debated together and approved on the same day in October 2014. In legislative debates, representatives in favor of the bill referred to equal rights, non-discrimination, and C189 (Blofield 2012; Poblete 2018).

In Chile, very few constitutional claims to women's equality are made in the courts. As one interviewee put it, "there really isn't a culture of claiming rights for discrimination. And there are not very good mechanisms for doing so either."[62] Moreover, when women do litigate, they use the statute, not the constitution, as the starting point. As a result, many employment-related cases in Chile concern dismissal without just cause, and most gender cases deal with pregnancy discrimination.[63] Generally, the questions raised do not require the application of constitutional law. For example, in *Maria Riesco Loyola v. Colegio Alicante del Rosal S.A.* (June 1, 2011), a female employee sought to have her dismissal by her employers during her maternity leave declared unjustified; on appeal, the Supreme Court upheld lower court rulings against the employer based on the labor code.[64] In a few cases, constitutional questions are raised. In *María Angela Salazar v. Universidad San Sebastián* (May 19, 2009), concerning the harassment and dismissal of a pregnant university professor and dean, the Court, on appeal, found that employers are limited by the constitutional rights of workers, particularly concerning their private lives and dignity.

Sexual and Reproductive Health

In this policy area, Chile and Argentina's legislation and process diverge more than they do in the other two policy areas. Reform in sexual and reproductive health has been very limited in Chile and generally has not been oriented toward gender equality. Argentina has passed more laws in this policy area, and the laws have been far more comprehensive.

Argentina

Although the Argentine Constitution does not have specific sexual health and reproductive rights provisions, constitutional rights have proven helpful to advocacy efforts. A researcher on sexual and reproductive health rights in Argentina clarified that:

> Precisely because of the Constitution, which introduced the strategies and language of Nairobi and the International Women's Conferences [etc.]; reforms such as the Sexual Health and Responsible Parenthood Law, the Comprehensive Sexual Education Law, the Law on Surgical Contraception, and emergency contraception were all based in these commitments.[65]

At the same time, conservatives have also used Article 75, Section 23 and the constitutional status of international treaties, particularly the American Convention on Human Rights and the Convention on the Rights of the Child, which recognize a right to life from conception.[66] The Supreme Court's interpretation of this provision is that it should not conflict with women's health and right to equality. However, conservatives, especially conservative judges in the lower courts, have referred to this treaty to justify their stance against contraception and abortion in all cases.

The language of women's constitutional rights, human rights, and international treaties that have constitutional status appear in most of the laws in this policy area as well as in legislative floor debates in Argentina. Legislators draw on arguments related to public health, the reduction of poverty, and the equality of men and women. However, they also frequently draw upon constitutional rights to make their case. In debates in the Senate and Chamber of Deputies on the Law on Sexual Health and Responsible Parenthood (No. 25,673/2003), legislators repeatedly referred to constitutional rights and the rights enumerated in international treaties.[67] In her opening statement introducing the bill, Representative Cristina Guevara argued that sexual health and responsible parenthood are basic human rights and that the state must ensure that citizens can fully exercise them. She went on to list all of the international treaties and conventions that pertain to this law, especially CEDAW and Article 75 Section 22 of the Constitution.[68] Representatives frequently cited equality of opportunity and women's rights as reasons to support the law.[69] Similarly, in the Senate, Senator Eduardo Menem cited constitutional rights and international treaties with constitutional status such as CEDAW, and he referred to comparative constitutional law in his arguments in favor of the Law on Sexual Health and Responsible Parenthood. Among other arguments, Menem noted that the right to sexual and reproductive health is already "consecrated" in CEDAW: "today all we are doing is regulating it."[70] Floor debates concerning the Law on Surgical Contraception, which entitles adults to tubal ligation or vasectomy through the health system, as well as the debates on the Law on Comprehensive Sexual Education, repeatedly refer to gender equality as provided in the Constitution.

Constitutional rights are also written directly into the text to justify the need for the law and to obligate the state to act. For example, Article 2 of the Law on Comprehensive Sexual Education and Article 4 of the Law on Sexual Health and Responsible Parenthood specifically refer to international treaties such as CEDAW and the Convention on the Rights of the Child, the constitutional rank of such treaties, and the need to bring education into compliance with these treaties and commitments. Importantly, these rights are also cited to require the state to ensure access to contraception and reproductive health care for all women. Thus, the Sexual Health and Responsible Parenthood Law not only removed legal bans to access but also obligated the state to fund these services. A national decree (No. 1.282/2003) issued soon after the legislation noted that the rights enshrined in international treaties and in Article 75 of the National Constitution required the state to "promote and implement positive action measures in order to guarantee the full enjoyment and exercise of the rights and freedoms" recognized therein. Similarly, the Law on Surgical Contraception also placed financial obligations on the state to ensure that surgical contraception is covered by insurance and provided free of charge.

Not surprisingly, these programs faced opposition in some provinces and significant opposition from conservative groups, especially the Catholic Church, that challenged aspects of the national health program in various domestic judicial venues (Piscopo 2014). In particular, legal challenges were lodged against the distribution of emergency contraception and sex education programs (ELA 2009, 269–270).

Abortion policy has followed a similar pattern: the Supreme Court has taken a relatively progressive approach grounded in constitutional rights and international law, but its decisions are routinely ignored by conservative judges and officials in the provinces. Article 86 of the National Criminal Code made abortion a criminal act in all cases except when the mother's health is at stake, or in the case of rape of a mentally incapacitated woman. In a landmark decision in 2012, the Argentine Supreme Court ruled that abortion was legal in all cases of rape, including for minors.[71] In the F.A.L. case, the Court argued that the interpretation of Article 86 needed to be consistent with international treaties that Argentina had ratified and thus had constitutional status. It went on to consider the pregnant woman's right to choose against the fetus's right to life. The Court ruled that Article 1 of the American Declaration of the Rights and Duties of Man and Articles 3 and 4 of the American Convention on Human Rights[72] were limited and must be balanced against the right to liberty, equality, and the dignity of every person; that "no absolute right to prenatal life exists" (Noguera 2019, 366). The Court further argued that Article 75 of the Argentine Constitution obligated the legislature to go beyond decriminalization and to take steps to ensure that women had access to abortion.[73] That is, the Supreme Court not only ruled that the state could not trample individual rights but also cited constitutional and international law to require the state to take proactive measures to ensure that women have access to abortion. Challenges from lower courts have significantly limited the impact of this ruling.[74] However, many of the same arguments made their way into the legislative debates a few years later.

Since the transition to democracy, over 50 legislative bills concerning abortion have been proposed; none made it to the floor for debate in the National Congress (ELA 2009, 276). In 2018, women's rights activists mobilized in large numbers to get abortion legalized for up to 14 weeks. The movement and the legislative debates generated conversations throughout the country. The Congressional debate for legalization mirrored many of the arguments made by the Supreme Court in the F.A.L. case and drew extensively upon the Inter-American Court of Human Rights ruling in Artavia Murillo v. Costa Rica. In Arta Murillo, the Inter-American Court ruled that the right to life shall be protected "in general" but that the embryo cannot enjoy the same rights as a person and that the right to prenatal life is not absolute. This decision was "constantly cited during Argentina's Congressional debate" (Noguera 2019, 379). Although the bill passed in the lower house, it failed in the Senate. Just as conservative groups, especially members of the Catholic Church, interfered with the implementation of the Sexual Health Law and the F.A.L. ruling, they were able to prevent reform of the abortion law. However, women's organizations continued to press for change, and just two years later, the bill was again put before Congress. In December 2020, abortion in the first 14 weeks was legalized, a "development [that] constitutes a transformation of historical proportions" (Sutton and Vacarezza 2021, 3).[75]

Chile

Chile has lagged behind other countries with respect to reproductive rights. In 1989, in the twilight of the authoritarian regime, abortion was criminalized.[76]

Other areas of reproductive health such as sterilization, education, and comprehensive access to family planning were already quite restrictive. Moreover, any discussion of reproductive health, particularly the decriminalization of abortion, sterilization, and the approval of the morning-after pill has been dominated by references to Article 19, No. 1 of the Chilean Constitution, which "protects the life of those about to be born."[77] As one health sector researcher explained, "in the areas of sexual and reproductive health, the Constitution makes it difficult to guarantee women's rights to reproductive health."[78] Policy change in the area of sexual and reproductive health has been limited. The Fertility Law and the legalization of abortion on some grounds are the two most significant laws in this policy area.

The Fertility Law (No. 20,418/2010) deals with sexual and reproductive health information, including emergency contraception. Proponents of this law drew upon the language of human rights and even women's rights far more often than they did in other legislative debates. For example, Representative Osvaldo Palma stated, "we're dealing with the freedom to choose, non-discrimination, the rights of women, the rights of families, the right to a free and informed decision as to when and how many children they want and can have . . . [we're dealing with] sexual freedom."[79] The law is limited to providing information about contraception and family planning to women and girls over 14 years of age. The most controversial aspect of the law is that it allows emergency contraception. Conservatives argued that it violated the Constitution and the right to life because it was abortive, while progressives and moderates did not engage Article 19, instead arguing that it was not abortive and thus not a violation of the Constitution.[80]

Chile was one of the six countries to ban abortion in all cases, and one of the strictest—women and doctors could be imprisoned for seeking or performing an abortion. Thus, decriminalizing abortion on three grounds was a milestone in women's reproductive rights. In 2017, the legislature passed a law partially decriminalizing abortion on three limited grounds: risk to the mother's life, fatal fetal malformation, and rape.[81] In the floor debates, legislators cited women's rights to equality, non-discrimination, dignity, privacy, and physical integrity in the constitution and international law. At the same time, conservatives challenged the constitutionality of the law on the grounds that it violated Article 19, No. 1, which protects the life of the unborn.

The Constitutional Court upheld the constitutionality of the law in a complex and divided decision.[82] In its reasoning, the majority states that questions regarding pregnancy and motherhood should be interpreted in the context of gender equality as it has been defined by the constitution, the legislative branch, and international law. It devotes significant space to constitutional and legislative changes that support gender equality, particularly the 1999 sex equality provision, and refers to developments in international law regarding gender-based violence and gender discrimination. Furthermore, the decision finds the legislature has reasonably balanced the fundamental constitutional rights of the mother with a legally protected interest in the potential life of the unborn. The Court's decision meant the law could be promulgated, decriminalizing abortion under limited circumstances. However, the decision also expanded the circumstances for the exercise of conscientious objection and may make it difficult to access the procedure (Maira, Casas, and Vivaldi 2019).

Chile and Argentina draw on the same international human rights treaties and case law to make a case for balancing a woman's rights against the rights of the fetus, and in some cases to argue that the woman's rights should win out. And yet, the outcomes are not the same. One notable difference is that Argentina's Supreme Court and the members of its legislature do not simply require the state to refrain from trampling individual rights but also take a proactive stance: "Argentine Constitutional law often places obligations on the state modeling itself after international human rights law" (Noguera 2019, 369). Both lawmakers and high courts require the Argentine state to take steps to ensure that citizens have access to services and benefits that the legislature has provided for in law. In contrast, Chilean laws do not obligate the state to ensure access to reproductive health services or to provide them free of charge through the healthcare system.

Conclusion

In this chapter, we consider the claims in the literature that link constitutional provisions to differences in processes and outcomes, focusing on legislation and high court cases from 1990 to 2020 in Argentina and Chile. Constitutional provisions are part of an institutional framework that may enable (or thwart) women's rights advocacy and shape the content of subsequent legislation. We expect that women's rights in the national constitution are reflected in processes such as policy change strategies, proposals, debates, and the legitimacy of rights claims. Constitutional rights can facilitate more favorable legislative and judicial outcomes.

Constitutional provisions do appear to enhance legitimacy and to be part of an enabling framework. Activists in Argentina repeatedly indicated that the constitutional gender provisions informed and assisted their efforts. In Argentina, advocates use the constitution to legitimize their claims, and the language of constitutional rights and equality is frequently used in debates, the text of the law, and court decisions. In particular, the presence of positive (or substantive) rights in the Constitution is frequently referenced in laws and judicial decisions that obligate the state, and even the private sector, to act.

Whereas in Chile, activists reported that the Constitution often thwarted their efforts; not one individual interviewed in Chile identified the Constitution as helpful. Although Chilean government officials or activists may at first justify legislation by referring to the equal rights provision, these references are often dropped, even by feminists, and the content of the law is subsequently weakened. The constitutional provision on family has dominated much of the discourse and is used to justify gender policy, even when the policy is directly related to women's rights. The supposed neutrality of the Constitution and the family provision appear to be obstacles to rights advocacy in Chile.

At the same time, the sex equality statement in the Chilean Constitution is not without meaning. Notably, some of the most progressive reforms in Chile have come after the 1999 sex equality provision was passed. In addition, while women's rights activists have had to counter conservative groups' often effective strategy of deploying the family provision, the equality provision has enabled them to achieve legislative changes such as the equal pay law. The sex equality provision appears to have been most useful in reversing or removing discriminatory legislation: "to [be able] say to those most opposed to gender advances . . . you can't be 'unconstitutional.' That's when it can be a powerful tool."[83] The sex equality provision also figured prominently in the Constitutional Tribunal's reasoning in the 2017 decision decriminalizing abortion.

Regarding the relationship between constitutional provisions and judicial outcomes, we found that gender discrimination cases are rare in both countries. In Argentina, having constitutional rights makes it possible to make rights-based claims and adjudicate them in the court system. Litigation is part of a multipronged strategy: constitutional provisions enable mutually reinforcing litigation, lobbying, and social mobilization strategies. As one scholar stated:

> the fight for justice is done on four legs . . . a case is put to a judge, it becomes an official public record and that serves to mobilize social movements, [it] serves as an "event" for the press to cover. Then, judges . . . have said that parliament needs to resolve the issue. [Ultimately] changes have come with legislation.[84]

The legal grounds for rights-based claims are more favorable in Argentina than in Chile. In the area of gender-based violence, for example, the high courts in Argentina are more apt to reference international law and regional agreements, resulting in a more developed national jurisprudence on gender equality. In Chile, however, very few constitutional claims to women's rights or equality are made in the courts. Activists can and do seek to legitimize rights claims using international law, but the lack of constitutional status and the uncertain legal position of international law in the legal hierarchy diminishes its usefulness (Vicuña and Bauzá 2005, 138–139). If Chile writes a new constitution that includes substantive equality, such provisions will enable rights advocacy and policy change.

Notes

1 This chapter draws extensively on an article previously published in the *Journal of Politics in Latin America* under the Creative Commons license CC-BY 4.0 (Lambert and Scribner 2021). Some of the interview quotations appear in an article previously published in *Politics, Groups and Identities* (Lambert and Scribner 2020).

2 The international networks include participation in international conferences such as the 1995 Fourth World Conference on Women in Beijing and Beijing Plus meeting, membership in regional networks such as the Latin American and Caribbean Committee for the Defense of Women's Rights (CLADEM) and the Organization of American States Commission on Women.
3 Argentina passed a 30 percent gender quota for legislative candidates in 1991. In 2017, Argentina passed the Gender Parity Law (27.412) requiring every other candidate on the party list to be a woman. In 2015, Chile enacted electoral system reform, which moved the country from a binomial system to an open list PR system and requires that no more than 60 percent of candidates in a district be of the same gender. During the period of study, Chile was well below world and regional averages for women's representation. The 2015 reform is helping to close this gap.
4 Renamed the National Ministry of Women and Gender Equality in 2016.
5 Interview with a prominent women's rights lawyer, Argentina, March 2011.
6 Article 75, No. 22 specifies several international human rights instruments that have constitutional status; CEDAW is one of them.
7 Interview with a prominent women's rights lawyer, Argentina, March 2011.
8 Interviews with a legislator and activist, women's rights scholar, women's rights NGO leader, gender-rights researcher, and member of the women's movement, April 2011.
9 Interview with a constitutional scholar, April 2011.
10 Interviews with lawyers of the Public Defender's Office, April 2011.
11 Interview with a prominent women's rights lawyer, March 2011.
12 Interviews with a legislator and activist, gender-rights researcher, women's rights scholar, member of the women's movement, and a prominent women's rights lawyer, and member of the women's movement, March and April 2011.
13 Interviews with a legislator and activist, and a prominent women's rights lawyer, March and April 2011.
14 Interviews with a legislator and activist, gender-rights researcher, and women's rights scholar, April 2011.
15 Interview with a prominent women's rights lawyer, March 2011.
16 Law 20.609 (2012) prohibits discrimination on the basis of sex, sexual orientation, and gender identity and provides a remedial complaint mechanism for victims of discrimination. However, the CEDAW Committee (2019) noted that the law does not include a comprehensive definition of discrimination against women.
17 Interviews with human rights constitutional law scholar, Ministry of Labor staff, and human rights NGO staff lawyer, March 2011.
18 Interviews with leaders and activists of a national human rights NGO, and a gender-based violence NGO, March 2011.
19 Ministry of Labor interview, March 2011.
20 Interviews with Ministry of Labor, human rights NGO staff lawyer, human rights NGO leadership, and Ministry of Health, March 2011.
21 Interview with a legislator, March 2011.
22 Interviews with legislators, SERNAM staff, and a lawyer for a Human Rights NGO, March 2011.
23 Interview with women's movement member, March 2011.
24 Vicuña and Bauzá (2005, 138–139) outline different views on the position of international treaty law in the legal hierarchy given the wording of Article 5 and the treatment of international law in the courts.
25 Interview with SERNAM staff, March 2011.
26 Interviews with constitutional law and litigation scholar, SERNAM staff, and a health sector researcher, March 2011.
27 UNHCR. 2014. "UN Working Group on the issue of discrimination against women in law and in practice finalizes country mission to Chile" Santiago de Chile

(9 September 2014). Available at: www.ohchr.org/EN/NewsEvents/Pages/DisplayNews.aspx?NewsID=15005&LangID=E.
28 Interview with a lawyer, academic, researcher and politician, March 2011.
29 Sanhueza, Anna Maria, "Los fallos y jueces que han impulsado la 'justicia de género.'" *Pauta*. March 8, 2019. Available at: www.pauta.cl/nacional/juzgar-con-perspectiva-de-genero-los-fallos-y-jueces-que-han-sido-clave.
30 Proyecto de ley "Modifica la Carta Fundamental que establece el deber del Estado de promover la igualdad de derechos entre mujeres y hombres." Available at: www.camara.cl/pley/pley_detalle.aspx?prmID=12272&prmBoletin=11758-07.
31 Chamber of Deputies session 51, July 31, 2018. Available at: www.camara.cl/pdf.aspx?prmID=13163%20&prmTIPO=TEXTOSESION.
32 The creation of the Women's Office of the Supreme Court of Argentina in 2009 has also contributed to this trend by focusing on cases involving women, training judges to incorporate a gender perspective, and increasing representation of women in the judiciary.
33 Versión Taquigráfica, Cámara de Diputados. Expediente No: 0250-S-2007. www.diputados.gov.ar/secparl/dtaqui/versiones/.
34 No. 26.791 Penal Code Addendum.
35 The circumstances surrounding the protests highlight the large gap between achievements in legal and policy reform on the one hand, and the complexity of implementation of gender policy on the other. See, for example, www.theguardian.com/global-development/sexual-violence.
36 For example, in B., M.P. v. G., R.A., a family court ruled in favor of an abused spouse citing Argentinian statutes as well as international human rights law. Legal Information Institute. Available at: www.law.cornell.edu/women-and-justice/location/argentina.
37 Interview with a prominent women's rights lawyer, March 2011.
38 This is based on the assessment of experts at Observatorio de Sentencias Judiciales. Available at: www.articulacionfeminista.org/a2/index.cfm?cnl=41&opc=9its.
39 Historia de la Ley 20.066, pp. 119, 172, 177. Available at: www.bcn.cl/histley/historias-de-la-ley-ordenadas-por-numero.
40 Interviews with leaders and activists of a gender-based violence NGO, and Ministry of Labor staff, March 2011.
41 UNHCR. 2014. "UN Working Group on the issue of discrimination against women in law and in practice finalizes country mission to Chile" Santiago de Chile (September 9, 2014). Available at: www.ohchr.org/EN/NewsEvents/Pages/DisplayNews.aspx?NewsID=15005&LangID=E
42 Interviews with leaders and activists of a gender-based violence NGO, March 2011.
43 In 2010, the Chilean penal code was amended to recognize the crime of femicide (Law 20.480).
44 See Karen González T. Santiago. "Critican fallo que acoge infidelidad como atenuante de femicidio," *La Tercera* (April 7, 2016). Available at: www.latercera.com/noticia/critican-fallo-que-acoge-infidelidad-como-atenuante-de-femicidio/.
45 Interview with women's movement member, Chile, March 2011. For example, in the case of *Lorenza Cayuhán* concerning obstetric violence while in state custody, the Supreme Court based its decision on Belem do Para, noting the rights of all women to live free from violence (para 13), including violence perpetrated by state authorities (CEDAW, para 14) (Supreme Court of Chile, Rol N° 92.795–2016 December 1, 2016).
46 Interview with SERNAM staff, March 2011.
47 Interview with a lawyer, academic, researcher, and politician, March 2011.
48 In addition to CEDAW, Argentina has ratified the ILO Discrimination (Employment and Occupation) Convention of 1958 No. 111 and the Equal Remuneration Convention of 1951 No. 1000. Furthermore, the Anti-Discrimination Law (23,592) specifically prohibits any discriminatory practice on the grounds of sex (and other categories).

49 See, for example, statements made by Senator Passo, Senator Paz, and Senator Barrionnuevo. Versiones Taquigrafica, Camara de Senado, Expediente No. CD 163/01. Available at: www.hcdn.gob.ar/secparl/dtaqui/versiones/. There was no debate in the Chamber of Deputies. Instead, the bill apparently was discussed in committee and went straight to the floor for a vote on November 27, 2001.

50 These ILO conventions provide a model for regulating domestic work including protection from abuse and harassment, regulation of work hours, annual paid leave, sick leave, and access to social security.

51 Interview with Ministry of Labor, Gender Equity/Equal Opportunity staff, April 2011.

52 Similar statements were made by Representatives Recalde, Giubergia, Iturraspe, on pp. 2–5 of the dictamine for the House of Deputies. Versiones Taquigrafica, Camara de Diputados, 3/13/2013. Expediente 0001-PE-2010. Available at: www.hcdn.gob.ar/secparl/dtaqui/versiones/.

53 There are no constitutional rights on gender and employment, but like Argentina, Chile has ratified ILO Convention No. 100 and CEDAW optional protocol which address workplace equality.

54 Moción Parlamentaria. Historia de la Ley N° 20.047. Available at: www.bcn.cl/historiadelaley.

55 Moción Parlamentaria. Historia de la Ley N° 20.005, p. 44.

56 Historia de la Ley N° 20.005, p. 351.

57 See, for example, *Jessica Oyarzún and Others/Promociones Financieras Ltda.* (January 14, 2009), and *Gisselle Maturana/Sociedad Comercial Maicao Limitada.* (March 18, 2009).

58 Moción Parlamentaria. Historia de la Ley N° 20.348, p. 7.

59 Interview with a legislator, and a journalist, March 2011.

60 Eduardo Diaz, Independent Regionalist Party. Historia de la Ley 20.348, pp. 77. Similar statements appear on p. 112 and p. 214. Available at www.bcn.cl/histley/historias-de-la-ley-ordenadas-por-numero.

61 One of the most significant weaknesses is that it does not ensure equal remuneration for men and women workers for work of equal value (the language used by ILO Convention No. 100). Interviewee members women's movement and journalists also criticized the equal pay law as being weak and favoring employers (March 2011). Moreover, under this law, it is not discriminatory "to pay a male employee more if he proves more suitable, qualified or responsible than his female counterparts." Marianela Jarroud "Many Chilean Women Keep Mum About Unequal Wages" *IPS News*. (August 2 2012). Available at: www.ipsnews.net/2012/08/many-chilean-women-keep-mum-about-unequal-wages/.

62 Interview with SERNAM staff, March 2011.

63 Chile's labor code prohibits dismissal of pregnant employees unless the employer can show serious misconduct.

64 Similarly in *Elizabeth Galaz Cuadra v. Fisco de Chile* (November 19, 2010) a woman who was dismissed from her position as a judge during pregnancy sought to be reinstated in her position. The Court upheld the dismissal on the grounds that judicial personnel are not covered by the labor law, but by a separate law.

65 Interview with a gender-rights researcher, April 2011.

66 Article 75, No. 23 states that Congress shall have the power to "enact a special and integral social security system that protects needy children, from gestation through the end of elementary schooling, and that protects the mother during pregnancy and nursing." For details on conservative strategies, see Defago and Faúndes (2014).

67 See, for example, Senator Muller on International Women's Conferences and the Convention on the Rights of the Child on pp. 4–5, Senator Menem on Article 75 of the Constitution, international law (especially CEDAW and the Rights of the Child), as well as international conferences and agreements including the World Conference on Population and Development in Cairo and the International Women's Conference in Beijing pp. 10–16 and p. 72–73, Senator Falco, p. 20–21, Senator Gomez de

Bertone p. 34. Versión Taquigráfica, Cámara de Senadores. Available at: www.senado.gob.ar/parlamentario/sesiones/busquedaTac.

68 Versión Taquigráfica, Cámara de Diputados. Expediente No: 1196-D-1999/0016-CD-2001. www.diputados.gov.ar/secparl/dtaqui/versiones/ p. 2.

69 For example, Deputy Silvia Marta Milesi of the Radical Civic Union (the UCR) saw the law as providing "equal opportunity" for poor women. Senator Mabel Caparros of the Justicialist Party (the PJ) stated, "adoption of this law is an achievement not only for women but also for men, because it means that citizens have access to the health care system on equal terms." Versión Taquigráfica, Cámara de Diputados, Expediente No: 1196-D-1999/0016-CD-2001.

70 Versión Taquigráfica, Cámara de Senadores, p. 11–12.

71 F.A.L. 2012. Originally, the law (1921) stated that abortion was legal for all three, but the changing of a comma in 1984 reduced the exceptions from these three to saving the woman's life or rape of an insane woman.

72 Article 4 of the American Convention on Human Rights states that "Every person has the right to have his life respected. This right shall be protected by law and, in general, from the moment of conception. No one shall be arbitrarily deprived of his life."

73 See the Court's note on *A. F. s/medida autosatisfactiva* at: www.cij.gov.ar/nota-8754-La-Corte-Suprema-preciso-el-alcance-del-aborto-no-punible-y-dijo-que-estos-casos-no-deben-ser-judicializados.html.

74 See "El aborto legal en Argentina: la justicia después de la sentencia de la Corte Suprema de Justicia en el caso 'F.A.L.'" Available at: www.ela.org.ar/a2/index.cfm?muestra&codcontenido=2147&plcontampl=43&aplicacion=app187&cnl=87&opc=53.

75 The law ensures that women can access an abortion through private or public health care providers and that a health care worker who obstructs or refuses to perform an abortion may be prosecuted and disqualified from practicing medicine.

76 From 1931 to 1989, abortion for medical purposes (to save the life or preserve the health of the mother) was legal. General Augusto Pinochet, in a conciliatory gesture to the Catholic Church, revised the penal code in 1989 as transition to democracy was imminent.

77 For example, in 2008, the Chilean Constitutional Tribunal "declared that the public health system's distribution of the pill was unconstitutional on the substantive grounds that this form of contraception can affect the constitutionally protected right to life of the fetus" (León 2014, 151). See *Requerimiento de inconstitucionalidad del Decreto Supremo N° 48 del Ministerio de Salud*. Rol 740–2007, Tribunal Constitucional April 18, 2008.

78 Interview with a health sector researcher, March 2011.

79 Historia de la Ley 20.418, pp. 97, 116.

80 Historia de la Ley No. 20.418. Available at: www.bcn.cl/historiadelaley/. A challenge in the Constitutional Tribunal was not successful. León (2014) offers a detailed account.

81 Known as the "Ley Que Regula La Despenalización De La Interrupción Voluntaria Del Embarazo" Law No. 21.030. Available at: www.bcn.cl/historiadelaley/nc/historia-de-la-ley/6701/.

82 See pages 76–79, and 98 of the full decision. Available at: www.tribunalconstitucional.cl/expediente?rol=3729wsdefrtg.

83 Interview with SERNAM staff, March 2011.

84 Interview with a health policy researcher, April 2011.

References

Alvarez, Sonia, Evelyn Dagnino, and Arturo Escobar. 1998. *Cultures of Politics, Politics of Cultures: Re-visioning Latin American Social Movements*. Oxford: Westview Press.

Asensio, Raquel. 2010. *Discriminación de Género en las Decisiones Judiciales: Justicia Penal y Violencia de Género*. Buenos Aires: Defensoría General de la Nación.

Blofield, Merike. 2012. *Care Work and Class: Domestic Workers' Struggle for Equal Rights in Latin America*. Penn State Press.

Blofield, Merike and Liesl Haas. 2005. "Defining a Democracy: Reforming the Laws on Women's Rights in Chile, 1990–2002." *Latin American Politics and Society* 47, no. 3: 35–68.

Craske, Nikki and Maxine Molyneux. 2002. "The Local, the Regional, and the Global: Transforming the Politics of Rights." In *Gender and the Politics of Rights and Democracy in Latin America*, edited by Nikki Craske and Maxine Molyneux, 1–31. New York: Palgrave Publishers Ltd.

Couso and Lisa Hilbink. 2011. "From Quietism to Incipient Activism: The Institutional and Ideological Roots of Rights Adjudication in Chile." In *Courts in Latin America*, edited by Julio Ríos Figueroa and Gretchen Helmke, 99–127. Cambridge University Press.

Defago, María Angélica Peñas and José Manuel Morán Faúndes. 2014. "Conservative Litigation Against Sexual and Reproductive Health Policies in Argentina." *Reproductive Health Matters* 22, no. 44: 82–90. DOI: 10.1016/S0968-8080(14)44805-5.

ELA (Equipo Latinoamericano de Justicia y Género). 2009. *ELA: Informe Sobre Género y Derechos Humanos en ARGENTINA (2005–2008)*. Buenos Aires: Biblos.

ELA (Equipo Latinoamericano de Justicia y Género). 2011. *Los Derechos de las Mujeres en la Mira: Informe Anual de los Observatorios de Sentencias Judiciales y de Medios—2010*. - 1ª ed.—Buenos Aires: Equipo Latinoamericano de Justicia y Género-ELA.

Franceschet, Susan. 2008. *The Politics of Domestic Violence Policy in Latin America*. University of Calgary: Institute for Advanced Policy Research.

Franceschet, Susan. 2010. "Domestic Violence Policy Outcomes in Chile and Argentina." *Latin American Politics and Society* 52, no 3: 1–29.

Franceschet, Susan and Jennifer Piscopo. 2008. "Gender Quotas and Women's Substantive Representation: Lessons from Argentina." *Politics and Gender* 4, no. 3: 393–425.

Gorban, Debora and Ania Tizziani. 2018. "Comparative Perspectives on Domestic Work in Latin America." *Journal of Latin American Studies* 9, no. 2: 4–18.

Irarrázaval, Luis Alejandro Silva and Jorge Ignacio Arab Massuh. 2014. "Legisladores y Jueces Frente a la Igualdad Constitucional de los Sexos." *Revista de Derecho Universidad Católica del Norte* 21, no. 1: 443–473.

Jaquette, Jane. 2001. "Regional Differences and Contrasting Views." *Journal of Democracy* 12, no. 3: 111–125.

Kohen, Beatriz. 2009. "The Effectiveness of Legal Strategies in Argentina." In *Feminist Agendas and Democracy in Latin America*, edited by Jane S. Jaquette, 83–112. Durham: Duke University Press.

Lambert, Priscilla A. and Druscilla L. Scribner. 2009. "A Politics of Difference Versus a Politics of Equality: Do Constitutions Matter?" *Comparative Politics* 41, no. 3: 337–357. www.jstor.org/stable/40599228.

Lambert, Priscilla A. and Druscilla L. Scribner. 2020. "Constitutions and Women's Rights Advocacy: Strategic Uses of Gender Provisions in Argentina, Chile, Botswana, and South Africa." *Politics, Groups, and Identities* 8, no. 2: 228–247. DOI: 10.1080/21565503.2018.1449759.

Lambert, Priscilla A. and Druscilla L. Scribner. 2021. "Constitutions and Gender Equality in Chile and Argentina." *Journal of Politics in Latin America* 13, no. 2: 219–242. Available at: https://doi.org/10.1177/1866802X211024245.

León, Fernando M. 2014. "Morning-After Decisions: Legal Mobilization Against Emergency Contraception in Chile." *Michigan Journal of Gender and Law* 21, no. 1: 123–175. Available at: https://repository.law.umich.edu/mjgl/vol21/iss1/3.

Lubertino, María José. 2003. "Pioneering Quotas: The Argentine Experience and Beyond." Presented at the The Implementation of Quotas: Latin American Experiences, Lima, Peru. Available via the IDEA at: www.idea.int/sites/default/files/publications/implementation-of-quotas-latin-american-experiences.pdf.

Maira, Gloria, Lidia Casas, and Lieta Vivaldi. 2019. "Abortion in Chile: The Long Road to Legalization and Its Slow Implementation." *Health and Human Rights Journal* 21, no. 2 (December): 121–131.

Noguera, Andrea F. 2019. "Argentina's Path to Legalizing Abortion: A Comparative Analysis of Ireland, the United States and Argentina." *Southwestern Journal of International Law* 25, no. 2: 356–392.

Piscopo, Jennifer. 2014. "Female Leadership and Sexual Health Policy in Argentina." *Latin American Research Review* 49, no. 1: 104–127.

Poblete, Lorena. 2018. "The Influence of the ILO Domestic Workers Convention in Argentina, Chile and Paraguay." *International Journal of Comparative Labour Law and Industrial Relations* 34, no. 2: 177–201.

Ríos Tobar, Marcela. 2007. "Chilean Feminism and Social Democracy From the Democratic Transition to Bachelet." *NACLA Report on the* Americas (March/April).

Ríos Tobar, Marcela. 2009. "Feminist Politics in Contemporary Chile: From the Democratic Transition to Bachelet." In *Feminist Agendas and Democracy in Latin America*, edited by Jane S. Jaquette, 21–44. Durham, N.C.: Duke University Press.

Ruibal, Alba. 2015. "Social Movements and Constitutional Politics in Latin America: Reconfiguring Alliances, Framings and Legal Opportunities in the Judicialization of Abortion Rights in Brazil." *Contemporary Social Science* 10, no. 4: 375–385.

Smulovitz, Catalina. 2010. "Judicialization in Argentina: Legal Culture or Opportunities and Support Structure." In *Cultures of Legality: Judicialization and Political Activism in Latin America*, edited by Javier A. Couso, Alexandra Huneeus and Rachel Sieder, 234–253. Cambridge: Cambridge University Press.

Sutton, Barbara and Nayla Luz Vacarezza. 2021. *Abortion and Democracy Contentious Body Politics in Argentina, Chile, and Uruguay*, edited By Barbara Sutton and Nayla Luz Vacarezza. London: Routledge.

Vargas, Virginia. 2002. "The Struggle by Latin American Feminisms for Rights and Autonomy." In *Gender and the Politics of Rights and Democracy in Latin America*, edited by Nikki Craske and Maxine Molyneux, 199–221. New York: Palgrave Publishers Ltd.

Vicuña, Francisco Orrego and Francisco Orrego Bauzá. 2005. "National Treaty Law and Practice: Chile." In *National Treaty Law and Practice*, edited by Duncan B. Hollis, Merritt R. Blakeslee and L. Benjamin Ederington, 123–154. Leiden: BRILL.

Waylen, Georgina. 2007. *Engendering Transitions: Women's Mobilization, Institutions, and Gender Outcomes*. Oxford, New York: Oxford University Press.

5

GENDER PROVISIONS, RIGHTS ADVOCACY, AND POLICY OUTCOMES IN BOTSWANA AND SOUTH AFRICA

Priscilla A. Lambert and Druscilla L. Scribner

> The language of the law wants to subsume everything under the term men like it is neutral, but then we said it "should be men and women" . . . in the founding document, the document that everyone would look at to say "what kind of South Africa did we want." [Then] when people think about human beings, they think about them in terms of them being men and women.
>
> —*Member of the women's movement, South Africa, Interview*

> The Constitution says we are equal, all equal. And I think that is the starting point of our lobbying and advocacy.
>
> —*Member of the women's movement, Botswana, Interview*

Introduction

The promise of constitutional gender equality provisions is the power to "include or exclude, to determine who has access to rights and resources and who falls within the boundaries of social and economic recognition/affirmation or beyond them in processes of exclusion, stigmatization and marginalization" (Albertyn 2005, 219–220). Are women included or excluded in a constitutional text; are they reflected in it and protected by it? As Williams has argued, constitutional provisions that "adopt a substantive model of equality rather than a formal one" promote gender equality (2009, 9). Regional neighbors South Africa and Botswana differ in the ways they include women and recognize gender equality in their respective constitutions. South Africa inscribes the principle of gender equality and an array of gender-specific rights in its Constitution, constitutionalizing

DOI: 10.4324/9781003303725-5

gender differences in an inclusive and egalitarian manner. Botswana's Constitution is neutral with respect to gender difference, though not wholly silent on sex discrimination.

This chapter draws on interviews with women's rights advocates and archival research on legislation, legislative debates, and high court decisions to illustrate how constitutional language that enumerates women's rights influences the content of legislation as well as judicial review of government policy. It also shows how a gender-neutral approach to women's equality can mask and perpetuate systemic disadvantages, particularly when cultural rights are entrenched. On the other hand, strong substantive gender equality provisions support efforts to attain and then later defend policy gains.

As a case study pair, South Africa and Botswana represent broadly different constitution types but share some features of interest in this study. For example, their legal systems share certain characteristics that are directly traceable to Roman-Dutch law (Himsworth 1974, 173). Both countries have plural legal systems with constitutional recognition of customary law, which affects women's rights in areas such as marriage, custody, property, and inheritance. They have similar exposure to regional and global intergovernmental processes and to transnational advocacy pressure to implement policies and create national gender machinery to improve the lives of women.[1] The international and regional context has had a profound effect on the policy content of local activism and the character of state institutions designed to support gender mainstreaming. Though the power, organization, and policy role of the state institutions dedicated to gender policy differ, the national gender machinery in both countries is committed to mainstreaming gender and promoting women's empowerment in national policy.[2]

South Africa and Botswana have significant political differences; most notably, South Africa has undergone the unique experience of apartheid and democratic transition. The South African women's movement, organized into the Women's National Coalition, exercised significant influence during the critical transition to democracy. Women's rights advocates participated in writing the Constitution and were instrumental in securing the inclusion of a strong gender equality commitment and other proactive provisions (Britton 2002, 41; Hassim 2002; Seidman 1999). The timing of the transition to democracy and the commitment of the left-leaning African National Congress (ANC) to gender and racial equality contributed significantly to public policy that affects women in South Africa (Waylen 2007b). Although a common purpose no longer unites the women's movement, rights advocates in South Africa work in a relatively favorable political climate with respect to several key factors associated with gender policy, especially the predominance of a left party in government and proportionally high numbers of women in parliament.[3]

In Botswana, in contrast, the conservative Botswana Democratic Party (BDP) has held power since independence and has strongly resisted pressures to accommodate gender equality reforms (Leslie 2006). In the mid-1980s, women organized to successfully fend off conservative attempts to further limit women's rights and have continued to pursue reforms to discriminatory legislation (Molokomme 1991; Van Allen 2000). Thus, unlike South African women, "Botswana women emerged on the political scene not based on an opening up of political systems by democracy but instead on account of a tightening of already restricted rights extended to women" (Geisler 2004, 166). Women's representation in national and local politics remains comparatively low. Just seven (11%) of the 63 elected seats in Parliament were held by women in 2019, whereas in South Africa, 185 of 396 (46%) seats in the National Assembly are held by women (Inter-Parliamentary Union). In addition to the constitutional differences, these divergent political circumstances affect the legislative climate in which gender policy is made.

Constitutional Provisions and Policy Change—Expectations

Following the theoretical expectations outlined in Chapter 2, we expect both process and outcomes to reflect the starkly different ways women's rights and gender differences are constitutionally recognized in South Africa and Botswana. Specifically, we anticipate that constitutional rights provisions concerning gender equality will affect how advocates use constitutional rights to challenge the status quo or defend legislative gains. Regarding the process, we expect rights provisions will serve as the basis for legitimizing a rights-based discourse, enable policy reform in the legislature, and provide legal tools and arguments that shape legal claims and their adjudication in courts. Likewise, we expect to find differences in policy outcomes such as legislation that enhances gender equality and high court decisions that either block or remove discriminatory laws or practices.

Enhances the Legitimacy of Rights Claims

Constitutional rights and duties reflect shared values and identity. A stated constitutional commitment to gender equality should increase the legitimacy of gender rights and ground arguments for gender policy change. We examine the congressional record to assess how constitutional provisions shape the language and discourse of the legislative process. We expect that gender equality and women's rights-based arguments are more likely to inform policy proposals in South Africa, where constitutional values pertaining to gender equality are explicit and obligate the state to address inequities. In both countries, the relationship between customary law and individual rights is expected to generate competing claims. In Botswana, where the foundation for gender equality is more limited, we expect to see greater reliance on international law arguments as a legal platform for gender equality.

Enables Policy Change

If constitutional gender provisions enable substantial legal reform, we expect policymakers and women's rights advocates in South Africa to identify egalitarian constitutional provisions as central to their advocacy strategies and to point up ways in which these provisions have enabled efforts to achieve policy outcomes such as legislative reform or alternatively prevented the political reversal of previous policy gains. In Botswana, we expect the limited and neutral recognition of gender in the Constitution to provide a weak anchor for women's rights-based policy change, whether through the legislature or the courts. Moreover, we expect that the constitutional relationship between customary law and non-discrimination will constrain the reform agenda of advocates in Botswana (Lambert and Scribner 2020).

Provides Legal Tools and Arguments That Facilitate Litigation

Constitutional provisions create or limit opportunities for rights-based litigation and affect the persuasiveness of rights-based arguments. Constitutional rights and obligations provide a legal foundation for argumentation, judicial interpretations of laws, and the protection and advancement of constitutional rights. In South Africa, a litigation approach to promoting gender equality is promising because the country takes a substantive approach to equality and provides legal standing for organizations in constitutional cases related to the public interest. We expect gender equality provisions to improve the opportunity to advance litigation on women's rights and improve the chances of women-friendly decisions in South Africa.

Comparing Constitutions

Across the two countries, we conducted 30 semi-structured interviews (19 in South Africa and 11 in Botswana) with individuals in several types of roles: leaders of non-governmental organizations, judges, lawyers working in legal advocacy organizations, prominent women's movement activists, former members of parliament, scholars and researchers working on women's issues and gender justice, and former and current government officials in ministries and commissions. These individuals helped write the constitution, directed key legal advocacy organizations, led litigation strategies and policy reform, or were involved in policy implementation.

In the first part of this case study, we review the gender equality provisions in each country and describe how interviewees view these provisions as informing and enabling their work and providing legitimacy to women's rights claims or mobilization. In the second half of the analysis, we consider gender provisions and policy outcomes in four areas: family and customary law, gender-based violence, sexual and reproductive health (SRH), and employment rights. We examine the discourse, content, and framing of key gender policy bills, committee and floor debates, and the text of the law. In our interviews with individuals engaged with policy development and implementation, we solicited their informed opinion about the legislative history, the strengths and weaknesses of specific policies, and their passage. Concerning litigation, we examined the record of high court decisions during the same timeframe and discussed litigation strategies and individual cases with our interviewees.

Part I: Gender in the Constitution

South Africa

Concerning substantive rights, the 1996 South African Constitution is one of the most inclusive in the world. It is the product of a unique democratic transition: it incorporates individual rights and a wide array of social and cultural rights; and it establishes a clear commitment to overcoming past injustices while recognizing diversity (Bauer and Taylor 2005, 249; Lambert and Scribner 2020). In the drafting and ratification processes, women lobbied for a constitutional principle of non-sexism and an equality clause that would supersede the right to custom and tradition. The Constitution includes the right to human dignity, a principle of non-sexism on par with non-racism, and a strong and substantive equality clause. Section 9 of the equality clause states that everyone is equal before the law and provides constitutional grounds for state actions to protect or help those disadvantaged by discrimination. Direct and indirect discrimination is prohibited on the grounds of race, gender, sex, pregnancy, marital status, ethnic or social origin, color, sexual orientation, age, disability, religion, conscience, belief, culture, language, and birth. As one scholar notes, "The inclusion of both sex and gender as grounds for proscribing discrimination protects women from invidious discrimination based on both biological and physical attributes, as well as social and cultural stereotypes about the perceived role and status of women" (Andrews 1998, 328). The mandate for affirmative action provides a foundation to address systemic disadvantages and constitutionally protects positive action from legal challenges.

The Constitution also details numerous rights of particular importance to women, including the rights to freedom and security of the person and bodily autonomy, freedom from violence, and reproductive choice, and contains a prohibition against any expression that amounts to advocating gender hatred. Section 7, No. 2 of the Constitution imposes a duty on the state to "respect, protect, promote and fulfill" enumerated rights, including equality, dignity, and freedom from violence. These are positive obligations, requiring the state to promote the realization of rights for individuals. The Constitution also requires courts to interpret legislation in the spirit of the Bill of Rights and to let international law and jurisprudence in other democracies guide judicial interpretation of the Bill of Rights (Section 39, No. 1 (b)).

The South African Constitution recognizes the right to celebrate traditional customs. It explicitly states, however, that customary law must be consistent with the Bill of Rights. Furthermore, the Constitution established the Commission for Gender Equality as a Constitutional body with a mandate to monitor and evaluate the implementation of gender policy and ensure the promotion of gender equality in both the private and public spheres.

In our interviews, advocates expressed that these constitutional provisions are essential, "the best tool," and have contributed substantially to their efforts to achieve policy change and engage in litigation.[4] For example, one legal advocate stated that "without a statement that affirms the need for gender equality, prescribed in fundamental law, the possibility to maintain gender rights in the broadest sense of those rights, not only in terms of women's rights, would be very difficult."[5] Others pointed to the importance of the Constitution's values and principles and the recognition of international law for constituting a national identity that includes gender equality: "The Constitution sets the baseline, it sets the agenda, it says 'this is what we aspire to be.' But it also gives South African citizens a tool to use if their rights are not being realized, to say 'but this is what our Constitution says.'"[6] While there is a yawning gap between the promise of gender equality in the Constitution and its practical realization, it provides a framework that can enable transformative change (Albertyn 2019b, 775). These views are echoed in South Africa's 2017 State Party report to the UN Economic and Social Council: "The Constitution acts as the normative foundation for the advancement of women's rights in South Africa, several pieces of legislation provide the building blocks."[7]

To clarify the view that the Constitution is part of an enabling framework, we asked advocates whether gender provisions were part of specific efforts to remove or reform discriminatory laws and whether they used these provisions to support their arguments in the courts or the legislature. Our interviewees indicated that gender-specific and socio-economic rights disproportionately affecting women were part of an enabling framework (Lambert and Scribner 2020). The Constitution allowed them to raise awareness, socialize leaders, gain media attention, and secure legislative changes and judicial decisions that would not have been possible otherwise. One individual who works on women's issues in other parts of Africa reflected that if the South African Constitution were different, "we would be hard-pressed to fight for certain rights, entitlements, and obligations."[8] For those working to secure policy change through lobbying and legislative efforts, gender provisions provided "leverage" to push for and win legislative change.[9] For example, Waylen (2007a, 537) contends that the reproductive rights clause in the Constitution was critical to achieving pro-choice legislation.

In the early 2000s, the pace of legislative change affecting women slowed (Albertyn 2005). Some women's organizations, such as the Centre for Applied Legal Studies and the Women's Legal Centre, pursued change through the courts. Those engaged in litigation identified the constitutional provisions and principles underpinning gender equality as central tools for their work.[10] Advocates used litigation strategies to raise awareness of women's rights and put relevant issues on the political agenda even when wins were unlikely. One South African lawyer described this strategy as "the art of losing a case."[11] Another confirmed that their organization would litigate "risky cases" if they promised to be high-profile cases that would help raise awareness of an issue.[12] The constitutional commitment to gender equality gives women's rights claims "a legitimacy that they did not have before" (O'Sullivan and Murray 2005, 40). Advocates have used constitutional rights to litigate against discriminatory laws, defend prior legislative gains, and hold the state accountable, including seeking damages in cases where the state failed in its constitutional duty.

Lawyers and judges highlighted the importance of specific provisions for providing legitimacy to legal claims in interviews.[13] One official emphasized that the "task of judging and the task of lawyering to promote gender equality is much easier when it's in the Constitution."[14] For the judiciary, "there's a real legitimate concern about inventing text that is not there. The Constitution provides strong arguments in support of equality to marshal in a relatively conservative society."[15] For judges tasked with applying the law, the Constitution makes the judge's job easier: "if the law is written down, is [explicit] and if the words are there, then 'well, what a relief'—it really does make life easy [for the judge]."[16] Several interviewees indicated that particular judicial decisions "would not have been possible if the Constitution didn't specify rights and obligate the state to act."[17]

Interviewees discussing litigation and legislative strategies emphasize the central importance of constitutional guarantees for protecting policy gains. Gender equality is "a very big card to put on the table. So that once a court realizes that they are dealing with gender issues and the characterization of the issue is clearly explained, there's not much possibility [for reversal]."[18] The Constitution sets the baseline in that all laws begin with the question of whether the law will pass constitutional muster. For example, "a private bill seeking to regulate abortion clinics was 'stopped in its tracks' when experts testified that it was unconstitutional."[19] Thus, even when the political climate is unfavorable (as it was, for example, during Jacob Zuma's presidency), constitutional rights are deployed as a critical backstop to prevent the erosion of women's rights.[20]

Finally, interviewees agreed that while international law can supplement and strengthen their arguments, it does not replace or supersede constitutional rights.[21] "The international commitments South Africa has made have filtered down quite a lot. But our Constitution speaks for itself . . . you just draw on international law to boost your argument."[22] These comments reflect a mixed approach to international law in the Constitution. While the Constitution incorporates customary international law[23] as domestic law, international agreements are not directly applicable. International commitments must be translated into national legislation to achieve the force of law.

Botswana

Botswana is one of Africa's few economic development success stories, with a relatively long history of political and economic stability. Its society and legal system, however, are highly discriminatory against women (Lambert and Scribner 2020). The country gained independence:

> as a bourgeois, bureaucratic state through a generally peaceful, colonially-mediated process, with no particular commitment to the emancipation of women beyond the right of suffrage and the same ambiguities about women's status embedded in its Constitution as could be found elsewhere in southern Africa.
>
> *(Van Allen 2000, 142)*

Botswana's Constitution was adopted in 1965 before the country held elections and achieved independence in 1966. At the time, "women did not feature in political parties much at all" and enjoyed few political or economic rights (Geisler 2004, 100).

The equality statement includes sex as one of several categories in Section 3: "every person . . . is entitled to the fundamental rights and freedoms of the individual, . . . whatever his or her race, place of origin, political opinions, color, creed or sex." Prohibition of discrimination, however, did not include sex as a category (Section 15). In *Attorney General of the Republic of Botswana v. Unity Dow*, the High Court and then the Court of Appeals interpreted the equality and discrimination clauses together as implying that the Botswana Constitution prohibits discrimination on the grounds of sex.[24] In the wake of *Dow*, the governing BDP proposed to amend the Constitution so discriminatory legislation could stand. The threat of amendment galvanized women's organizations and focused advocacy efforts on reforming discriminatory legislation (Leslie 2006). The *Dow* decision provided the basis for a 2006 constitutional amendment to the non-discrimination clause that included sex among the categories in Section 15.[25]

In Botswana, the constitutional recognition of equal treatment and non-discrimination is an important mechanism by which women can challenge sex-based discrimination. As a result, women's rights advocates recognize their Constitution as both important for challenging sex discrimination and limited in its ability to inspire substantive or transformational legal change. Landmark cases discussed in this chapter, such as *Dow v Attorney General* and *Mmusi v Ramantele*, confirm the role of constitutional litigation and judicial review in fighting discrimination against women in Botswana. While these few judicial decisions are prominent and promising, women in Botswana lack "effective, accessible and enforceable protection from discrimination" (International Commission of Jurists 2013, 54).

For women, one of the most critical aspects of Botswana's Constitution is that while it guarantees fundamental rights, it simultaneously states that customary laws are exempt (Fombad 2004). Customary law governs family law matters: marriage and divorce, rights within marriage, division of shared property, inheritance, and child custody. For example, a woman has no right to her husband's property upon his death. The Botswana Constitution specifically excludes customary law from the equality and non-discrimination provisions. Before the 2005 amendment adding sex to the non-discrimination clause, government officials maintained not only that sex discrimination did not violate the Constitution but also that "the omission of sex in the non-discrimination clause was intentional and was made in order to permit legislation in Botswana which was discriminatory on grounds of sex" (Fombad 2004, 144). As one interviewee noted, "We have a Bill of Rights that says nobody must be discriminated against but then in the same Constitution you have a protection of customary law that says when it is custom it is not discriminating."[26]

None of the interviewees mentioned using the Constitution as a tool in their efforts to secure policy changes. One lawyer and politician reported: "I'll tell you what, we have never made a reference to the national Constitution."[27] The director of a human rights NGO made a similar statement; their organization had never "taken a matter forward using the Constitution and gender issues."[28] Interviewees suggested that gender equality arguments have not been a winning strategy for litigators, though one lawyer viewed the Constitution as "sufficient" as long as the judges are progressive.[29]

While the Constitution is not enabling, some interviewees said the sex equality statement provides a baseline.[30] Advocates have drawn on the lone equality provision to argue for the revision of explicitly discriminatory laws and to oppose new legislation that would violate the principle of equality before the law. Policy successes in Botswana have been mostly limited to removing discriminatory legislation. In 1997, following the *Dow* decision and sustained pressure by activists, the government of Botswana established a commission of inquiry to review all laws discriminating against women, which resulted in law reform in some areas, though not necessarily immediately. The Abolition of Marital Power Act (2004), discussed in the section on family and customary law, is an example of reform to address tangible acts of discrimination (Sechele 2022). No proactive measures have been enacted to increase women's political or economic power.

Advocates in Botswana draw upon international law as much as possible: "We have a constitution, but the Constitution is a very outdated constitution . . . So what to do? We are looking at international commitments."[31] The Constitution of Botswana contains no provision delineating the role of international law within the national legal order. International law references and arguments have met with resistance from judges and lawmakers.[32] One activist recounted how they used international law arguments, including the argument that the government had ratified CEDAW and that it is public policy. However, when they encountered judicial resistance and skepticism, the constitutional argument was their main argument.[33] Others were more pessimistic, stating that there is little possibility of affirmative or positive actions for gender equality in Botswana, regardless of its international commitments.[34] Recent judicial decisions indicate greater reliance on international law argumentation and an increased acceptance of human rights and gender equality jurisprudence. The Botswana High Court's decision in *Mmusi v Ramantele* discussed later in the chapter is a case in point.

Overall, interviewees in Botswana characterized the Constitution as a hindrance to gender equality efforts and voiced a desire for changes to the Constitution.[35] The most common wish we heard was for the domestication of international law. Ten years later, constitutional review and revision are on the political agenda. In 2022, a Presidential Commission of Inquiry (the Dibotelo Commission) began a process to examine whether the Constitution of Botswana should be reviewed. Women lobbied for and succeeded in gaining nearly equal representation on the Commission, which is holding a months-long public consultation process across the country. This process opens the door for women's groups to identify weaknesses and suggest potential revisions supporting gender equality. The Dibotelo Commission was slated to make its recommendations to the President at the end of September 2022.

Part II: Gender Policy

In this section, we compare legislative reforms and judicial decisions in four gender policy areas: family and customary law, gender-based violence, SRH, and employment rights. We pay particular attention to laws and court decisions that address common issues or appear similar in content in both countries to clarify how policy changes are related to the way gender is constitutionalized. In South Africa, legislation, policy debates, and reforms often reflect the constitutional commitment to gender equality and are more likely to obligate the state to act to fulfill constitutional guarantees. In Botswana, the government has tended to pursue gender-neutral policies, "avoiding the use of such words as men, women, girls, boys, father and mother in prevalence to phrases such as 'households,' 'citizens,' 'their staff,' and 'government officers'" (Kalabamu 2006, 241). The policy reform achievements in Botswana have mostly involved the removal of discriminatory laws and policies; none have been proactive measures to increase women's political or economic power. In both countries, litigation is part of the strategy for achieving policy change and has been crucial in challenging overtly discriminatory policies and practices, particularly with respect to customary law.

Family and Customary Law

Customary law has been identified by women's groups as a particularly contentious area of law, and conflict between rights and culture "often plays itself out on the bodies of women through harmful cultural practices" (Gouws and Galgut 2016, 8). Women's movements across Africa have pursued a rights-based strategy in challenging customary law, particularly with respect to land tenure and inheritance (Tripp 2004). Both countries accept customary law and common law. However, constitutional recognition of customary law is very different in Botswana and South Africa. In both countries, there have been important court cases and laws passed, but South Africa goes much further to protect women's rights in marriage and property.[36]

South Africa

Section 31 of South Africa's Constitution recognizes the right to celebrate traditional customs but explicitly states that customary law is subject to the Constitution and must be consistent with the Bill of Rights. These constitutional conditions guided the passage of the 1998 Recognition of Customary Marriages Act.[37] The Act removed inequality in customary marriages and abolished husbands' status as guardians. A memorandum on the act explains that the motivation of the law is to reconcile the constitutional principle of preserving African cultural traditions with the right to equal treatment and non-discrimination.

The Bill of Rights provisions on equality and rights against unfair discrimination have been used to challenge customary law with respect to inheritance and distribution of property. In *Bhe v. Magistrate, Khayelitsha and Others (2004)*, the South African Constitutional Court found that a rule about male primogeniture in African customary law entrenched patriarchy and violated women's constitutional guarantees to human dignity and equality. The Court argued not only that the customary law in question was inconsistent with the Constitution but also that customary law in general must evolve to meet new community standards.[38] In *Shilubana and Others v. Nwamitwa (2008)*, a case concerning the succession of community leadership, the Court recognized that customary law could evolve to promote gender equality.[39]

In *Gumede v. President of the Republic of South Africa and Others (2008)*, the Court confirmed a Durban High Court ruling that gender discrimination in the division of property in divorce proceedings cannot be justified by customary law and is unconstitutional on gender equality grounds. Mrs. Gumede challenged a rule that women could not own property under customary law as codified in the KwaZula-Natal province. The Court declared provisions in Section 7, No. 1 of the Recognition of Customary Marriages Act regulating property division inconsistent with the Constitution.[40] The subsequent 2009 Reform of Customary Law clarifies the law concerning succession for widows and children born out of wedlock who are not sufficiently protected by customary law.[41] In the 2017 *Ramuhovhi and Others v President of the Republic of South Africa and Others* judgment, the Court found that differentiating between pre-Act polygamous marriages and new polygamous customary marriages amounted to unfair discrimination.[42]

On the other hand, policy progress on the legal recognition of Muslim marriages has stalled. A Muslim Marriages Bill was introduced in 2010 to address the inequalities resulting from the non-recognition of these marriages, but the legislation did not advance.[43] In 2014, the Women's Legal Centre initiated a constitutional challenge against the state's failure to pass legislation recognizing and legalizing Muslim marriages. In its decision in *The President of RSA v Women's Legal Centre Trust* (December 2020), the Court of Appeal highlighted that "non-recognition of Muslim marriages is a travesty and a violation of the constitutional rights of women and children in particular, including their right to dignity, to be free from unfair discrimination, their right to equality and to access to court."[44] The Constitutional Court heard oral arguments in August 2021 but had not yet issued a ruling at the time of this writing.[45]

Because the Constitutional Court may provide the legislature with a timeframe to enact legislative change to address the constitutional defect in law as part of its judgment, the policy implications of successful litigation are clear. Yet the litigation processes themselves can also raise awareness and foment social mobilization in favor of the legislative change. For example, in *Jezile v. S and Others*, the perpetrator appealed his conviction (22 years) by claiming that bride abduction, or ukuthwala, was a cultural practice governed by customary law. The court upheld his sentence and argued that "culture and tradition cannot justify such practices that clearly violate constitutional rights to dignity, freedom of choice, security of the person and education." This case helped publicize the practice of ukuthwala and the violation of women's rights. It motivated a public outcry that resulted in a government-commissioned report recommending legislation to ban forced and child marriages (UN Human Rights Council 2016, 7).

Explicit constitutional provisions supporting gender equality have been critical in preventing the erosion of women's rights in this area, particularly as the political climate shifted unfavorably under Jacob Zuma's leadership of the ANC and his presidency. Jacob Zuma became president of the ANC in 2007 and President of the Republic in 2009 with the backing of traditional leaders whose power had been waning. During his bid for power, Zuma was embroiled in rape and corruption charges, of which he was acquitted. According to one of our interviewees, "following the Zuma rape trial and Zuma's acquittal for rape, there was a sense that men now had the right to discipline women."[46] Politically, a deeply resentful and conservative discourse about women emerged along with "a kind of backlash frame."[47] With respect to policy change, interviewees reported they "were backtracking. We've stagnated, and we're actually going backward."[48]

The long and fraught legislative history of the Traditional Courts Bill illustrates how women's groups use the legal tools afforded by the Constitution to counter conservative legislation and prevent backsliding. The bill concerns the status of the traditional justice system and navigates the relationship between customary law and the Constitution. It has a long history rooted in ANC politics. The Traditional Courts Bill was introduced in 2008; it was withdrawn in 2011 and then quietly revived at the National Council of Provinces in 2012 with no changes. Women's groups were vocal and organized in their opposition, arguing that the bill "would reinforce patriarchal power relations and potentially reverse some of the positive changes women have managed to win" since the transition to democracy (Claassens 2009, 18).[49] Public comments on the Traditional Courts Bill submitted to Parliament in 2008 and 2012 emphasized key issues affecting women that violated their constitutional rights (Weeks 2011; Thipe 2013).[50] As one former MP shared, "Having that Constitution is giving us so much more strength and power to raise these issues wherever they raise their ugly heads."[51] The 2008/2012 bill failed to pass in the upper house after five of nine provinces refused to support it in 2014.

In 2017, an improved version of the Traditional Courts Bill was introduced that included an "opt-out" clause to allow individuals to bypass customary courts. However, traditional leaders lobbied to abandon the opt-out clause because it undermined their power (Osman 2018). The version of the bill without the opt-out provision passed the National Assembly in 2019 and the National Council of Provinces in December 2020.[52] Opposing the bill in the National Council of Provinces, Ms. Labuschagne, a representative from the Western Cape, stated, "Any province that supports equal rights for women and children and any province that champions our constitutional principles and the rule of law cannot reasonably support this Bill."[53] The lack of an opt-out provision is arguably unconstitutional. The Traditional Courts Bill was returned to the National Assembly for a concurring vote, and the National Assembly sought constitutional review before proceeding with the passage.

Botswana

As noted previously, Botswana's Constitution exempts customary law from the equality and non-discrimination provisions (Section 15, No. 4 (c) and (d)).[54] As a result, women in Botswana have few legal grounds to challenge customary laws. The women's movement has fought hard to address legal discrimination in family law and subsume customary law to women's equal rights, but with few advances (Van Allen 2007).

One attempt to address inequality in marriage was the Deeds Registry (Amendment) Act of 1996. This amendment allowed married women to hold property in their own names. The amendment bill was part of a larger effort by the ruling BDP to "remove policy and legal impediments" that hinder women. Support for the bill in parliamentary debate reflected a shared appetite for reform. For example, Mr. Gabaake of the BDP opined, "I do not think there is anyone in this house who would oppose such a bill. We have to accept that our laws have been discriminatory in many ways and have put a number of women in a disadvantage." Hon. Kokorwe of the BDP stated on the floor, "for many years women married in community of property have suffered in silence, they owed nothing [. . . and had] always been treated as a minor and that must come to a full stop." Mr. Kavindama of the opposition saw the bill as a way to "get rid of [abusive] behavior from husbands" and "ensure that a husband must be responsible for his family."

However, the legal entrenchment of marital power was so pervasive in Botswana that it undermined gains in family law reform. The women's movement considered the issue of marital power a significant stumbling block in the pursuit of their goals. As a prominent member of the women's movement stated in an interview:

> Marital power just simply said the male person was king, and so he had the power to decide whether you can still walk into the bank and get a loan without his consent. So even [though] your income, your salary is part of that estate, you can't just borrow because you have income. He has to give consent. And so after celebrating, we realized we had run very fast but not run far.[55]

Marital power subjects the wife to the husband's guardianship, effectively giving her the status of a minor. South Africa abolished marital power through the Justice Laws Rationalization Act No. 18 of 1996. In Botswana, Parliament passed the Abolition of Marital Power Act in 2004. The Abolition of Marital Power Act legally ended "the power of men as household heads and sole decision-makers in family property and other related issues" (Alexander 2005, 34). It is an excellent example of legislative reform of overtly discriminatory law and was intended to bring Botswana's marital property regime in line with what was happening elsewhere in southern Africa at the time (Sechele 2022).

A significant weakness of the 2004 Abolition of Marital Power Act is that customary and religious marriages are excluded from its application. Tradition and culture were key arguments against the passage. Chiefs and Parliamentarians opposing the abolition of men's marital power "argued that 'men are natural heads of households and decision-makers' which should not be questioned" (Alexander 2005, 35). Some members of Parliament argued that the Bill was "out of step with Tswana tradition" (Quansah 2005, 26). For example, Pono Moatlhodi, Member of Parliament (MP) for Tonota South, insisted that abolishing marital power was an insult to "nature's way of family life," went "against the bible," and was "against the tradition and culture that had 'always held people tightly together'" (cited in Sechele 2022, 130–131).

The High Court supported an interpretation of the Abolition of Marital Power Act as limited by customary law until the *Mmusi v Ramantele* decision.

Edith Mmusi and her sisters challenged the rule of Ngwaketse customary law that denies women the right to inherit a family residence that forms part of their late father's estate.[56] In 2010, the Customary Court of Appeal ruled that the estate should pass to their nephew and ordered Mmusi to vacate the family home. Mmusi appealed to the High Court of Botswana in Gaborone in 2012. The judge ruled in her favor, finding that the customary rule in question violated the right to equality. The decision draws on comparative law developments in customary inheritance laws in Ghana, Kenya, India, Nigeria, South Africa, and Tanzania as well as international instruments regarding gender equality that Botswana has signed (Jonas 2013, 236).[57] The High Court judgment illustrates how international law can supplement and support arguments in favor of gender equality in the absence of substantive constitutional rights.

The nephew Ramantele and the Customary Court of Appeal (represented by the Attorney General) appealed the judgment in 2013.[58] Their arguments centered on the maintenance of tradition and the constitutional position of customary law. Ultimately, the Court of Appeal found "that customary law should be interpreted to include the family home passing to women" (Weinberg 2016, 197).[59] The decision from the country's highest court was the first to affirm gender equality under customary law and was hailed as a landmark. The 2014 Married Persons Property Act was passed in the wake of this decision. It allows persons married under customary law to opt for civil law to administer their properties.

Additional legislative change affecting women's ability to own property came recently when the National Assembly approved the Land Policy in 2019. The new law, which took effect in 2020, amends the 2015 Land Policy, which prevented married women from owning land independently if their husbands already owned land. The revision deleted a stipulation that only one spouse could apply for land. The new law reflects an equal treatment approach: Either individual can now apply for land. This was an important win for married women's equality. Nevertheless, like Botswana's other gender-neutral laws, the measure is silent about affirmative or positive action for women, a group that has historically been excluded from direct ownership and control of land in Botswana (Kalabamu 2021, 5).

Gender-Based Violence

The rates of violence against women are high in both South Africa and Botswana, though official statistics are not widely available. In Botswana, a 2012 study conducted by Gender Links found that "nearly one-third of women (29%) experienced Intimate Partner Violence in the past 12 months," and nearly 70% had experienced violence in their lifetime (Machisa and van Dorp 2012). In South Africa, a 2011 prevalence study in Gauteng by Gender Links and the Medical Research Council found that "more than half of women have experienced gender-based violence" (UN Human Rights Council 2016, 4). The two countries are consistently in the World Population Review's top 10 ranking of countries with the highest rates of rape worldwide.

Botswana and South Africa take different constitutional approaches to women's rights and state obligations regarding violence against women. South Africa's Constitution states that all citizens have an "inherent dignity and the right to have their dignity respected and protected." The "freedom and security of the person" recognized in Section 12 of the Constitution includes the right to be free from all forms of violence from public or private sources and the right to bodily and psychological integrity. The Constitution of Botswana includes a provision for the protection of "life, liberty, security of the person and the protection of the law." However, due to the lack of a substantive constitutional commitment to gender equality in Botswana, the individual right to personal security has not been a powerful argument or anchor for anti-violence policy. Legislative reforms and legal activism to address violence against women in each country have reflected these differences.

South Africa

South Africa's 1998 Domestic Violence Act[60] resulted from the political and legal gains that women made during the transition to democracy as well as sustained legal advocacy that "use[d] law to legitimize a focus on women's rights" and achieve legal reform (Hunter 2006, 66). The preamble of the legislation characterizes domestic violence as a serious social problem and recognizes that the state has a responsibility to end violence against women and children. It invokes the Constitution (the right to equality, freedom, and security of the person) and international commitments (CEDAW). The law was groundbreaking at the time. It defines domestic violence in broad terms (including physical, economic, and emotional abuse, harassment, and intimidation), specifies policies, procedures, and obligations (and disciplinary measures if police fail to meet these obligations), and details court powers and procedures. The implementation of the Domestic Violence Act lagged due to insufficient budgets, inadequate training, complexity, and lack of agency coordination. These problems inspired a coordinated advocacy campaign for the implementation of the Act (Usdin et al. 2000).

Additional legislative efforts in this policy area include the 2007 Sexual Offences Amendment Act,[61] which criminalizes all non-consensual sexual activity, including marital rape, and brings sexual violence and related offenses and crimes under one statute with consent at the center. The 2011 Protection from Harassment Act and the 2013 Combating Trafficking in Persons Act also address gender-based violence. Despite constitutional protections and these policy changes, violence against women and girls is widespread and normalized. The implementation of the policy remains uneven; there is low police compliance with the Domestic Violence Act, limited access to coordinated state services, and a legacy of structural violence (Spies 2019; Britton 2020).

Women's rights advocates have used litigation to strengthen the implementation of existing laws, hold the police services accountable, and provide greater oversight of the public services responsible for addressing gender-based violence. The Sexual Offences Amendment Act has been revised several times in response to successful litigation. For example, a 2012 amendment addressed judicial discretion in sentencing after an appeal of a 2009 sexual assault case exposed a legal loophole.[62] In that case, the Supreme Court of Appeal stated that:

> Our Constitution sets its face firmly against all violence, and in particular sexual violence against vulnerable children, women and men. Given this, and the Act's emphasis on dignity, protection against violence against the person, and in particular the protection of women and children, it is inconceivable that the provision could exonerate and immunize from prosecution acts that violated these interests.[63]

The *Levenstein* case (2018)[64] and the subsequent 2021 amendment to the Sexual Offences Amendment Act highlight how advocates can use women's constitutional rights litigation to push forward women-friendly legislative change. The controversy centered on Section 18 of the Act, which distinguished between rape/compelled rape and other sexual offenses, such as sexual assault, that were considered less serious and, therefore subject to a statute of limitations.[65] The applicants, adult survivors of childhood sexual violence, challenged the constitutionality of this distinction. They argued that distinguishing rape or compelled rape from other forms of sexual offenses is "irrational and arbitrary" and that selectively providing protection on this basis violates survivors' "rights to human dignity, equality, and non-discrimination, to be protected from abuse as children, to be free from all forms of violence from both public, and private sources, and access to courts" (para 9). The applicants also argued that "sexual abuse in all forms, not only rape, infringes the survivor's right to bodily and psychological integrity" and that the "state has a duty in terms of Section 7, No. 2 of the Constitution to respect, promote and fulfill this right" (para 27). These arguments were bolstered by a friend of the court briefs from the Women's Legal Centre and the Centre for Applied Legal Studies, among other organizations. The High Court and Constitutional Court agreed with these arguments and declared the provision constitutionally invalid. The Constitutional Court provided the legislature with 24 months to amend the law and an interim corrective "reading-in" of Section 18 that would become permanent if Parliament failed to act, thus pushing legislative change forward.

The judgments outlined earlier build on case law in which the Constitutional Court has reinforced gender equality provisions and affirmed the state's obligation to take proactive measures to ensure women enjoy the right to freedom from violence. For example, in *S v. Baloyi* (2000), the Court found that the state has a duty "to protect the right of everyone to be free from private or domestic violence" and that the state has a constitutional and international obligation to "deal with domestic violence" (para 11 and 13).[66] In *Carmichele v. Ministry of Safety and Security* (2001), the Court found the Constitution and international law obligate the "state to protect the dignity and security of women" and thus that the state has a positive duty to protect women.[67] In *F v. Minister of Safety and Security (2012)*, the Court drew upon *Carmichele* to argue that the minister was vicariously liable for the rape of a 13-year-old girl by a police officer on "stand-by" duty. The Court reasoned that the state is responsible for protecting the public in general and women and children in particular.[68] The decision goes further to highlight how violence against women violates "interlinked fundamental rights treasured by our Constitution," including "privacy, dignity and self-worth, freedom, and the right to be treated with equal regard" (para 55). Citing *Carmichele* (para 37), the judgment reiterates that violence against women goes to the "very core of the subordination of women in society . . . entrenches patriarchy [and] imperils the freedom and self-determination of women" (para 56).

Violence against women is a key issue area in which the Constitution's gender provisions are used in feminist struggles in the courts, in Parliament, and in the streets to change law, create a shared understanding about gender-based violence, and acknowledge gender inequality publicly. This is evident in the September 2019 protests that erupted in front of Parliament and on social media under the hashtags #NotInMyName #AmINext and #SAShutDown in response to a wave of violence against women. Standing in front of Parliament, activist Lucinda Evans yelled to protestors, "If this government fails to protect us, we, as the women of South Africa, will take them to the Constitutional Court."[69] In response to the protests, President Ramaphosa addressed an urgent joint sitting of Parliament and the National Council of Provinces, the first such joint sitting since 2005, and declared gender-based violence a national crisis.[70] The Government introduced three bills in 2020 to address violence against women: the Criminal Law (Sexual Offences and Related Matters) Amendment Bill, the Criminal and Related Matters Amendment Bill, and the Domestic Violence Amendment Bill. These bills were passed in 2021 and signed into law in 2022.[71]

Botswana

In Botswana, little progress has been made on gender-based violence law beyond revising the penal code and passing the Domestic Violence Act. In 1998, the penal code was revised to broaden the definition of rape, make it gender-neutral, and provide protections for all victims of sexual violence, as well as minimum sentences for convicted offenders (with higher sentences for HIV-positive offenders).[72] The gender-neutral language about sexual offenses criminalizes same-sex offenses (Tabengwa and Nicol 2013).[73] Botswana passed the Domestic Violence Act in 2008. The Act defines domestic violence as "any controlling or abusive behavior that harms the health or safety of the applicant." Implementation of the act has been hampered by the problems seen elsewhere: police reluctance to get involved in what is seen as trivial family matters, referral to customary courts, and pressure on women to drop cases (International Commission of Jurists 2013, 77).[74] The Public Service Act, passed the same year, included the first legislative prohibition of sexual harassment. It applies to public sector employees only. Both pieces of legislation are limited.

National law in Botswana does not recognize marital rape, nor do the courts. For example, in a 2003 court case brought by a woman who was abducted and repeatedly raped by her husband, the judge ruled that marriage implied consent. Moreover, customary law allows a man to "chastise" his wife (Selolwane 1998). Since customary law courts may hear domestic violence cases, it can be difficult to address sexual violence in the family, especially in rural areas. The government has been engaging with Dikgosi (chiefs) to address these kinds of issues. In 2015, the Dikgosi adopted an Action Plan on Mainstreaming Gender and Addressing Gender-Based Violence in their communities that included establishing Gender Committees at the district level. Just two such committees had been established in 2018.[75] Marital rape and domestic partner exceptions in law imply the state's consent to discriminatory laws and customs that systematically disadvantage women and contravene international law (Scribner and Lambert 2010).

The CEDAW Committee recommends that Botswana revise the Domestic Violence Act and the Penal Code and develop a law on gender-based violence that would bring the country in line with international and regional human rights commitments.[76] In 2018, Parliament passed the Penal Code Amendment Bill, which introduced stronger penalties for rape and raised the age of consent from 16 to 18. In his 2018 State of the Nation Address, the President pledged support for two bills: a Sexual Offences Bill and a Sex Offenders Registry. The Sex Offenders' Registry Act was passed in 2020; however, a sexual offenses bill that would have brought together fragmented legal provisions related to rape and sexual violence did not advance.[77] These legislative efforts focus on stiffer penalties for offenders and naming and shaming perpetrators to address gender-based violence. President Masisi touted the reforms as appropriate for a "society of chivalry where males were gentlemen; a society where uncles were protective guardians; where fathers were cushions and cloaks of security for the homestead."[78]

Botswana's Constitution does not obligate the state to protect women's rights or ensure freedom from violence. High Court cases on gender-based violence focus on punishing the perpetrator. *State v. Matlho* (2008) is an example.[79] As noted earlier, the penal code was revised to include minimum sentences for rape with severer punishments when the perpetrator is HIV-positive. In *Matlho*, the Botswana Court of Appeal upheld concurrent sentences for the HIV-positive perpetrator of two rapes. The judgment found that the punishment was not unconstitutional and noted the need to send a "strong and clear message that the courts will ensure that such protection [for women] is afforded by the sentences on those who violate women's rights." Similarly, in *Sekoto v. Director of Public*

Prosecutions (2007), the Court of Appeal upheld the prison sentence for a man who murdered his girlfriend and argued that the courts should impose stiff penalties as a deterrent, as such cases were increasing.

Sexual and Reproductive Health

This section examines the cross-national differences between South Africa and Botswana concerning women's legal rights and ability to exercise agency in their reproductive lives. It also highlights how rights advocates use the available legal tools to promote and defend reproductive rights and sexual health. The challenge of addressing high rates of HIV transmission in a context of high gender-based violence has shaped SRH policy and comprehensive sexuality education in both countries. Both have significant gender disparities in HIV infection rates.[80] South Africa and Botswana also have similar rates of unintended pregnancies (65% and 66%, respectively) and unintended pregnancies that result in abortion (37% and 32%, respectively).[81] Here we focus on abortion policy, which allows us to compare how constitutional provisions inform legislation and provide advocates with tools to push for better SRH policy implementation and defend policy gains from conservative efforts to rescind them.

South Africa

The South African Constitution states in Section 12 that everyone has the "right to bodily and psychological integrity," including "the right to make decisions concerning reproduction" and "security in and control over their body." Section 27 states that "everyone has the right to access health care services, including reproductive health care." South Africa has also "ratified all the relevant international human rights instruments that ground SRH as human rights," including the Maputo Protocol (Berro and Durojaye 2019, 56). Article 14 of the Maputo Protocol guarantees women's right to health, including SRH, and obligates state parties to take all appropriate measures to "protect the reproductive rights of women by authorizing medical abortion in cases of sexual assault, rape, incest, and where the continued pregnancy endangers the mental and physical health of the mother or the life of the mother" (Article 14(2)(c)).

The Choice on Termination of Pregnancy Act, 92 of 1996, was one of the first post-apartheid laws to support gender equality. Replacing the 1975 Abortion and Sterilization Act was a campaign issue for the ANC in the 1994 elections. Supporters of legal reform faced organized opposition from religious and professional groups and the National Alliance for Life. Groups supporting the ANC-led reform effort included the Women's Health Project, the Abortion Reform Action Group, and the Reproductive Rights Alliance, among others. They framed "abortion access as a means for creating greater gender equality as well as furthering women's rights" (Guttmacher 1998, 193).[82] At the time of its passage, the Act was intended to "widen access to safe, legal abortion" and affirm "women's moral autonomy, personhood and bodily integrity" (Albertyn 2019a, 105).

The Choice on Termination of Pregnancy Act was initially successful in addressing maternal mortality from unsafe abortion: "annual deaths in public facilities from unsafe procedures fell by 91% soon after the 1996 law" (Guttmacher 2017, 33). However, the long-term implementation of the law has been challenging for reasons familiar to other gender policy areas. These include:

> state inaction (e.g., failure to provide information, designate and staff clinics, procure drugs) and an absence of formal rules (e.g., no guidelines or protocols in place), as well as powerful and oppositional informal practices (especially around stigma, moral judgments, and conscientious objection).
>
> *(Berro and Durojaye 2019, 57)*

These issues and the general inefficiency of public health services severely reduce access to legal family planning and abortion services. The Act was amended in 2004 and 2008 to address issues of accessibility and help reduce maternal mortality from unsafe abortion.[83]

The Choice on Termination of Pregnancy Act has endured for over 25 years, withstanding "attempts to strike it down in the courts and to dilute its provisions in Parliament, as the Constitution has been mobilized to support reproductive rights" (Albertyn 2019a, 105). A court challenge to the law was launched within a year of its passage. In *Christian Lawyers' Association of South Africa and Others v. Minister of Health and Others* (1998), the plaintiff challenged the constitutionality of the Choice of Termination of Pregnancy Act on the basis of fetal personhood.[84] Armed with constitutional reproductive rights, women's rights organizations developed an innovative legal strategy to defend the law and joined as co-defendants (Albertyn 2005, 223).

The High Court ruled that Section 11 of the Constitution protecting the right to life of everyone was not intended to protect a fetus. Furthermore, the court accepted the arguments of those defending the Act. The judgment notes that the Constitution is "primarily an egalitarian constitution, and that transformation of society along egalitarian lines involves the eradication of systemic forms of domination and disadvantage based on race, gender, class and other grounds of inequality." Affording legal personality to the fetus would impinge on women's constitutional rights to equality, freedom and security, dignity, life, privacy, religion, belief and opinion, and health care.[85]

In another failed attempt to weaken Choice on Termination of Pregnancy Act, *Christian Lawyers' Association v. The Minister of Health* (2005), the plaintiff challenged the constitutionality of sections of the law dealing with informed consent.[86] The Act advises but does not require parental consent for minors and does not include an age bar. The High Court found the informed consent provisions to be consistent with the Constitution and the most appropriate requirement in light of the foundational principle of self-determination that underpins the right to terminate a pregnancy. A woman's self-determination, the Court argued, is guaranteed by the constitutional rights to bodily and psychological integrity, access to reproductive health, dignity, and privacy (Pickles 2012).

Legislative challenges to reproductive rights fail the constitutional test and thus have not passed the committee stage. For example, in 2007, Ms. Cheryllyn Dudley of the African Christian Democratic Party (ACDP) presented the "Constitution Seventeenth Amendment Bill (The Right to Life of the Unborn Child)" with the objective of amending Sections 11 and 28 of the Constitution to ensure reasonable protection of the right to life of the unborn child.[87] This bill failed, and in 2017, Ms. Dudley introduced a new Choice on Termination of Pregnancy Act Amendment Bill that included additional barriers to access, such as a requirement for a consultation with a social worker, an ultrasound, and mandatory counseling (Berro and Durojaye 2019).[88] This bill was rejected by the Portfolio Committee on Health in 2018. In committee, Ms. P Kopane of the Democratic Alliance argued that the Bill was fatally flawed: "From a constitutional perspective, the proposed Bill places an unnecessarily heavy burden on those who wish to terminate a pregnancy. Read with the Bill of Rights; it does not allow freedom of choice."[89]

While the constitutional protections are strong, women still face institutional, economic, and cultural difficulties in accessing legal abortion services in South Africa. As a result, Berro and Durojaye (2019) argue that "South Africa has fallen short" of complying with international standards (68).

Botswana

There are no constitutional provisions concerning health generally or SRH specifically in Botswana. Additionally, of all the SADC member states, only Botswana and Madagascar have failed to ratify the Maputo Protocol. Sexual and reproductive rights policies have focused on free family planning services and sex education in and out of school (State response to CEDAW 2019). Abortion was criminalized comprehensively until 1991 when an amendment to the Penal Code allowed for legal abortion under limited circumstances in the first 16 weeks of pregnancy.[90]

Compared with South Africa, access to safe and legal abortion is restricted. The procedure requires the approval of two medical doctors and must be carried out by a registered medical practitioner in a government hospital, registered private hospital, or approved clinic (Botswana Penal Code, Article 160). The mobilization for the 1991 Penal Code (Amendment) Bill decriminalizing abortion procedures under limited circumstances came from the medical community. The revision to the criminal law protected the medical community but fell "far short of increasing women's control over their bodies" (Mogwe 1992, 42).

Given the limited legal grounds for abortion, the regulations affecting access, and the conservative culture in Botswana, women with unwanted pregnancies and HIV-positive women may resort to illegal and potentially unsafe abortions. Underreporting and secrecy make it difficult to accurately collect data on abortion in Botswana (Mogobe, Tshiamo, and Bowelo 2007). Yet post-abortion complications are among the top three causes of maternal death in Botswana (Nkhwalume and Mashalla 2019), and complications from abortion are the leading cause of maternal death in the first trimester of pregnancy (Ngwako and Banke-Thomas 2020, 30). Despite the clear consequences for maternal health, the legalization of abortion is not on the political agenda.

Rights-based advocacy for SRH care is weak due to cultural attitudes about women's sexual and reproductive autonomy and the lack of an enabling legal framework for claiming rights. Smith (2013) argues that women in Botswana do not claim rights and do not see the law as accessible to them because they have internalized their subordinate status. In Botswana, law is for men; for women to have, claim, and exercise individual rights is to be gendered as male. As a result, "women exercising rights as women is just not possible" (Smith 2013, 48).[91] Women's legal and social subordination to men and factors such as poverty and intergenerational sexual relationships are primary explanations for consistently higher rates of HIV infection for women compared to men (Phaladze and Tlou 2006).

Workplace Equality

Recognizing and promoting gender equality and equal opportunities in the workplace, including equal pay, is central to achieving greater social and economic equality for women. In South Africa and Botswana, rights advocates pursuing workplace equality have starkly different legal tools. South Africa's constitutional commitment to ensuring gender equality and overcoming past discrimination is combined with a strong gender-specific non-discrimination clause as well as gender-neutral employment rights to fair labor practices that bolster efforts to level the playing field for women. In Botswana, the equality statement and non-discrimination clause provide a basis for a right to equal treatment in the workplace. The Constitution includes no explicit employment rights, gender neutral, or otherwise. These differences between the two countries are reflected in their levels of employment equity, their sexual harassment policies, and their histories of employment litigation.

South Africa

South Africa's equality provisions (Section 9) prohibit anyone from discriminating directly or indirectly on the grounds of gender, sex, pregnancy, and marital status. Additionally, discrimination on any of these grounds is presumed to be unfair. These provisions have informed the country's labor law. South Africa's 1998 Employment Equity Act explicitly prohibits unfair discrimination based on race, gender, sex, pregnancy, and marital status. The Employment Equity Act directly reflects the commitment to gender equality and positive actions to remedy past discrimination. Specifically, the legislation's preamble states that the objective is to "promote the constitutional right of equality and the exercise of true democracy." The Act also provides for positive action to remediate inequalities in the workplace in order "to promote equal opportunity through elimination of unfair discrimination [and] implement affirmative action measures to redress . . . disadvantages" (Chapter 1, Section 2).[92]

The Employment Equity Act includes extensive details on the prohibition of discrimination, positive action, monitoring, enforcement, and legal proceedings. Moreover, it places the burden on the employer to prove that the discriminatory action was fair. Pregnancy discrimination is also addressed in the Labour Relations Act (1995)—Section 187 prohibits the dismissal of an employee for any reasons related to her pregnancy. Dismissal on the grounds of pregnancy is automatically considered unfair. Maternity leave is legislated through the Basic Conditions of Employment Act (1997), which requires four months of maternity leave around the time of childbirth.

Discrimination claims are adjudicated in specialist Labor Courts, which reinforce the Employment Equity Act and the Labor Relations Act and regularly draw upon the constitutional rights to equality and fair labor practices. In *CWIU v. Johnson and Johnson Ltd.* (1998), the Labor Court found that a series of layoffs was discriminatory because the only jobs not targeted for layoffs were jobs open only to men (Scribner and Lambert 2010). In *Lukie v. Rural Alliance CC* (2004), an employee was told not to return to work after the birth of her baby.[93] The Labor Court found this dismissal to be related to her pregnancy and hence automatically unfair under the Labor Relations Act. In *De Beer v SA Export Connection CC* (2008), the Labor Court upheld a right to full legal maternity leave.[94] In its judgment, the Labor Court found that "Section 187(1)(e) of the Labor Relations Act must be seen as part of social legislation passed for the specific protection of women and to put them on an equal footing with men." In *Mashava v. Cuzen and Woods Attorneys* (2000), the Labor Court ruled that an employee (including a probationary employee) cannot be required to disclose her pregnancy status. An exception to the protection against pregnancy discrimination is *Woolworths v. Whitehead* (2000), in which the Labor Court of Appeal overturned a pregnancy discrimination judgment, finding that the employer's actions were not based on a requirement of job continuity and were not related to pregnancy.[95] The decision was controversial because it opened the door to employer arguments that a requirement of job continuity could be a prerequisite for employment.

South African law also addresses sexual harassment generally and in the workplace. Generally, claims of sexual harassment can be pursued via the constitutional rights to fair labor practices. The Protection from Harassment Act of 2011 defines sexual harassment widely and includes stalking behaviors and electronic harassment that violate the individual's constitutional right to privacy and dignity.

Concerning sexual harassment in employment specifically, Section 6 of the Employment Equity Act specifies that "harassment of an employee is a form of unfair discrimination and is prohibited on any one, or a combination of grounds of unfair discrimination." A separate "Code of Good Practice on the Handling of Sexual Harassment Cases" defines sexual harassment, employer liability, and legal remedies. The Code was amended in 2005 to reflect the Constitution and the discrimination framework of the Employment Equity Act. Echoing the Constitution's equality statements and the constitutional rights underpinning the Act, the Code recognizes sexual harassment as a form of unfair discrimination based on sex, gender, and/or sexual orientation.[96] The amendment brings sexual harassment "within the realm of discrimination and the right to be free from sexual violence and discrimination within South Africa" (LRC 2010, 7). The Employment Equity Act also makes these rights actionable via employer liability, including vicarious liability, for sexual harassment. Additionally, courts may award damages, given that harassment harms an individual's right to dignity (Mogapaesi 2019). In *Ntsabo v. Real Security CC* (2003), the Labor Court found that an employer could be liable for the actions of their employees when they were aware of the harassment and failed to act appropriately.[97]

Overall, employment regulations that define and address discrimination, pregnancy discrimination, and sexual harassment in South Africa use the language of gender equality and the constitutional commitment to it. A final example is the Promotion of Equality and Prevention of Unfair Discrimination Act, 2000 (Act No. 4 of 2000), which applies to all employment issues excluded from the Employment Equity Act. The law makes affirmative action mandatory, giving effect to Section 9 of the Constitution, and relies on the Equality Courts for enforcement.

Botswana

In Botswana, the 1982 Employment Act regulates employment relations in the private sector, whereas the 1998 Public Service Act regulates public sector employment. The Employment Act is generally gender-neutral and includes no provisions related to harassment. It has been amended several times in ways that affect female workers and shore up gender-neutral language. For example, the 1996 amendment eliminated protections for female employees that restricted night work and working underground in mines. Section 23 (d) of the Employment Act states the prohibited grounds of discrimination, which include race, tribe, place of origin, social origin, marital status, gender, color, creed, and disability. A 2010 amendment added sexual orientation and health status to these grounds. Section 23 has been used to challenge unfair dismissal on the grounds of sex and pregnancy. In *Moatswi v. Fencing Centre (Pty)* (2002), for example, the Industrial Court found that an employer had engaged in indirect discrimination by dismissing a group of women on the basis that they were not suited to the requirements of the occupation, which involved heavy lifting and night shifts. The employer was found to have discriminated on the basis of sex in violation of Section 23 and ILO conventions signed by Botswana.[98]

The Employment Act provides a maternity leave of 12 weeks, including a six-week confinement before birth and a six-week leave post-birth for female employees. Employees may not be terminated due to pregnancy and must be allowed to take maternity leave. During this time, employers must pay them 50% of their salary if the employees comply with the strict procedure for requesting leave. In *David v. Auto & General Supplies*, the Industrial Court found that an employer who had terminated a female employee upon her return from maternity leave had failed to prove that her dismissal was unrelated to her pregnancy or childbirth and thus had engaged in unlawful discrimination.[99]

Botswana's Employment Act prohibits gender-based discrimination in dismissal only; it does not affect other employment decisions, such as hiring and promotion. Thus, with respect to pregnancy, the Act "does not protect female job seekers from discrimination based on their reproductive function" and "remains silent on the [ILO Maternity Convention] prohibition of requirements to undergo pregnancy tests by job applicants and females who have already been absorbed into the labor market" (Mogapaesi 2022, 70).[100]

The scope of Botswana's Employment Act is limited, especially when compared with South Africa's Employment Equity Act. In Botswana, the Employment Act includes no mention of positive (affirmative) action, sexual harassment, or other gender issues, and enforcement is reported to be weak in the private and informal sectors (Alexander 2005, 17). At the time of its most recent CEDAW review, Botswana reported plans to review the Employment Act to "include provisions on equal pay for women and men for work of equal value and the prohibition of sexual harassment" (2019 CEDAW Report para 35).[101]

In the area of sexual harassment, the comparison with South Africa illustrates the shortcomings of the approach taken in Botswana. In Botswana, the Public Service Act recognizes sexual harassment in the workplace between public sector employees, but there is no equivalent in the private sector.[102] The silence of the Employment Act on sexual harassment "leaves employees uncertain of the existence of legal recourse or the availability of remedies against perpetrators" (Mogapaesi 2019, 348). A Code of Good Practice provides some guidance for employers and employees in addressing sexual harassment in the workplace, but employers are not obligated to implement the suggested policies. Nor does the legal framework on sexual harassment in Botswana meet its international law obligations (Mogapaesi 2019, 440). In South Africa, in contrast, where the law is grounded in constitutional rights, employers and employees have explicit rights and face known legal procedures. This clarity and comprehensiveness allow for "laws to be tested and developed further before the courts" (Mogapaesi 2019, 452).

Conclusion

Several lessons stand out from the Botswana—South Africa case study. Across the four issue areas examined in this chapter, legislation in both countries reflects constitutional ideals and concrete provisions concerning gender equality. In each policy area, the differences between the two countries in legislative outcomes are related to the way gender is treated in the constitution. In South Africa, the legislation is more specific in its objectives, scope, and methods of enforcement than the legislation in Botswana. Moreover, the legislation reflects the tenor of the equality clause, recognizing that gender-based discrimination is pervasive and structural. Legislation regulates both public and private domains in which women experience discrimination: in intimate relationships, in their families, in their working relationships, in the market, and so forth. South African courts have vigorously upheld the constitutional concept of substantive gender equality and worked to balance gender equality against other constitutional values.

Botswana's gender-neutral Constitution has limited activists' ability to push for policies that promote women's equality and redress systemic gender discrimination. However, the sex-equality statement and the 2006 non-discrimination provision have played an important role in efforts to remove overt discrimination in laws and policies. The disadvantage of this neutral approach is that equal treatment can mask and perpetuate systemic disadvantages. In the case of land policy, for example, Kalabamu (2006, 244) argues that adopting gender-neutral policies in Botswana has not empowered women but instead acted to "conceal women's exclusion from land resource management and ownership."

Another lesson is that egalitarian provisions are central to defending policy gains. For example, as the political environment became hostile to women's equality in South Africa, constitutional rights provided a critical tool to prevent backsliding. The enumeration of rights, in the words of one of our interviewees, "means it's not so easy to reverse the gains [we have already achieved], and if they are reversed, we can run back to the Constitution and say 'we are going against the Constitution here, this is what the Constitution says.'"[103]

Compared to their counterparts in South Africa, Botswana's rights advocates, legislators, and judges face a much less favorable legal framework for advancing and protecting women's rights. As a result, such actors are more likely to rely on international law to support their arguments. The *Mmusi v. Ramantele* case illustrates the role of international law when there are few constitutional rights that advocates and judges can draw upon.

The clawback clause for customary law in Botswana is an enormous obstacle to women claiming their rights. It also places courts at the forefront of the effort to balance competing constitutional claims. In turn, this situation puts the High Court and the Court of Appeals under pressure "to turn either to creative legislative interpretations, as seen in the *Dow* case, or avoid applying some provisions of the Constitution altogether, as seen in the *Ramantele* case" (Dinokopila and

Kgoboge 2021, 356). These decisions expose the courts to criticism that they are reaching beyond their role, potentially harming their legitimacy in the long term. In contrast, in South Africa, lawyers and judges involved in women's rights litigation need not engage in judicial overreach by inventing text that is not there. Dinokopila and Kgoboge (2021, 357) argue that the courts' approach in Botswana is laudable in its support for human rights; however, it is:

> not sustainable, and has led to questions concerning the consistency of the courts in the resolution of disputes. [Moroever, the approach] has contributed to the delay in effecting constitutional reforms in the country as there is an unfounded belief that the constitutional framework adequately protects women and children from discriminatory customary law practices.

It also leaves women's rights dependent upon the presence of progressive judges.

Finally, across the four policy areas—but particularly in the case of violence against women—constitutional rights, legislative advances, and court-won policy changes do not easily or immediately translate into tangible improvements for women. Rates of violence against women remain very high in both countries. In South Africa, where the Constitution and the legal framework for addressing violence are arguably very strong, the persistence of high levels of gender-based violence points to enormous gaps between the promise of rights in law and their realization (Britton 2020; Albertyn 2019b). It bears repeating that this book is not intended to address this gap, nor does the existence of a gap between rights and practice mean that rights do not matter. Rather, rights are a tool, best used in combination with other tools to chip away at the foundations that underpin systemic, pervasive, and structural discrimination against women.

Notes

1 Regional commitments with gender provisions include the Constitutive Act of the African Union, the African Charter on Human and Peoples' Rights, and Southern Africa Development Community (SADC) Protocol on Gender and Development. South Africa has also ratified the Protocol on the Rights of Women in Africa. At the international level, both are signatories to the UN Convention on the Elimination of All Forms of Discrimination Against Women (CEDAW), the Optional Protocol to CEDAW, the Beijing Declaration and Platform for Action (BPFA), and the Universal Declaration of Human Rights.

2 The National Gender Machinery (NGM) in South Africa is complex and overlapping; some bodies have been dismantled over time, while others are under-resourced and fragmented (Gouws 2004; Gouws and Madsen 2021). The constitutionally required Commission on Gender Equality has the mandate to advocate for gender equality and monitor outcomes. In Botswana, the Women's Affairs Department (WAD) was located in the Ministry of Labor and Home Affairs. In 2016, the Ministry was renamed the Ministry of Nationality, Immigration, and Gender Affairs.

3 Prior to the first multiracial elections held in 1994, the South African Parliament had less than 2.7% representation of women. The proportion of women in office increased

to 27% following these elections and saw additional increases over the years attributable to the adoption of a gender quota by the governing ANC.

4 Interviews with a former member of parliament and member of the women's movement, member of the Commission on Gender Equality, and a scholar and researcher, July 2012.

5 Interview with a Human Rights Commission lawyer, August 2012.

6 Interview with a former member of parliament and member of the women's movement, July 2012.

7 Consideration of reports submitted by States parties under Articles 16 and 17 of the International Covenant on Economic, Social, and Cultural Rights. Initial reports of States parties due in 2017 — South Africa (April 25, 2017), Document E/C.12/ZAF/1 dated June 7, 2017.

8 Interview with a scholar and researcher in July 2012.

9 Interviews a legal scholar and advocate at a litigation-focused NGO, a former ANC MP and member of the women's movement, a scholar and researcher, and a scholar and former member of the Commission on Gender Equality and member of the women's movement, July 2012.

10 Interviews with a member of the judiciary, a constitutional law scholar, a lawyer at a litigation-focused NGO, and a Human Rights Commission lawyer, July and August 2012.

11 Interview with a scholar and advocate at a legal advocacy NGO, July 2012.

12 Interview with a lawyer at a litigation-focused NGO, July 2012.

13 Interview with a Human Rights Commission lawyer; Interview August 2012.

14 Interview with a member of the judiciary, July 2012.

15 Interview with a member of the judiciary, July 2012.

16 Interviews with a constitutional law scholar, and a member of the judiciary, July and August 2012.

17 Interviews with a Human Rights Commission lawyer, a lawyer at a litigation-focused NGO, and a scholar and advocate at a legal advocacy NGO, July and August 2012.

18 Interview with a member of the judiciary, July 2012.

19 Interview with a legal scholar and advocate at a litigation-focused NGO, July 2012. This bill is discussed later in the chapter.

20 Interviews with a former member of parliament and member of the women's movement, a lawyer in a litigation-focused NGO, a legal scholar and researcher, a member of the judiciary, and a constitutional law scholar, July and August 2012.

21 Interview with a lawyer at a litigation-focused NGO, staff at the Department of Justice, a member of the judiciary, and a former member of parliament and member of the women's movement, July 2012.

22 Interview with staff at the Department of Justice, July 2012.

23 Customary international law refers to international obligations that arise from established and accepted international practices. Other obligations arise from formal international treaties or conventions.

24 *Dow v. Attorney General* 1991 BLR 233 (High Court); *Attorney General v. Dow*, 3 July 1992 (Court of Appeal). The case concerned a 1982 citizenship law and became the focal point for women's organizations in the 1990s and 2000s (Molokomme 1991; Van Allen 2000).

25 Constitution Amendment Act No. 9 2005. Section 15.3 states: "the expression 'discriminatory' means affording different treatment to different persons, attributable wholly or mainly to their respective descriptions by race, tribe, place of origin, political opinions, color, creed or sex."

26 Interview with a member of the women's movement, July 2012.

27 Interviews with a lawyer, and a politician with the BCP, July 2012.

28 Interview with a human rights leader, July 2012.

29 Interview with a lawyer and women's rights activist, July 2012.
30 Interview with members of the women's movement, July 2012.
31 Interview with a human rights leader, July 2012.
32 Interviews with a member of the women's movement, a human rights leader, and a lawyer and women's rights activist, July 2012.
33 Interview with a lawyer and women's rights activist, July 2012.
34 Interview with members of the women's movement, July 2012.
35 Interviews with a lawyer, a politician with the BCP, a human rights leader, and members of the women's movement, July 2012.
36 Similarly, a clear connection can be drawn between constitutional changes affecting women's rights and status in the Ugandan Constitution (1995) and subsequent legal mobilization of women's groups centered on reform and policy change affecting customary law (Tripp 2004).
37 The Recognition of Customary Marriages Act, 1998 (Act No. 120 of 1998) came into force in November 2000.
38 *Bhe v Magistrate Khayelitsha* 2005 (1) BCLR 1 (CC) available by name at the court's website: www.constitutionalcourt.org.za.
39 Shilubana v. Nwamitwa 2008 (9) BCLR 914 (CC); 2009 (2) SA 66 (CC).
40 *Gumede (born Shange) v. President of the Republic of South Africa and Others* (CCT 50/08) [2008] ZACC 23; 2009 (3) BCLR 243 (CC); 2009 (3) SA 152 (CC) (December 8, 2008).
41 The Reform of Customary Law of Succession and Regulation of Related Matters Act, 2009 (Act 11 of 2009) came into effect on September 20, 2010.
42 *Ramuhovhi and Others v President of the Republic of South Africa and Others* (CCT194/16) [2017] ZACC 41; 2018 (2) BCLR 217 (CC); 2018 (2) SA 1 (CC) (November 30, 2017).
43 Available at: https://static.pmg.org.za/bills/110117muslim-marriages-bill.pdf.
44 *President of the RSA v Women's Legal Centre Trust; Minister of Justice and Constitutional Development v Faro; and Minister of Justice and Constitutional Development v Esau (Case no 612/19) (2020) ZASCA 177 (December 18, 2020)*.
45 *Women's Legal Centre Trust v President of the Republic of South Africa and Others* CCT 24/21.
46 Scholar, former member of the Commission on Gender Equality, and member of the women's movement; Interview July 2012.
47 Scholar, former member of the Commission on Gender Equality, and member of the women's movement; Interview July 2012.
48 Attorney, litigation-focused NGO, Interview July 2012.
49 The Women's Legal Centre along with other NGOs formed the Alliance for Rural Democracy to lead a public campaign to defeat the bill.
50 Constance Mogale, "Traditional Courts Bill: Rural Women's Access To Justice Is Betrayed Again." *Daily Maverick,* February 16, 2021. Available at: https://www.dailymaverick.co.za/article/2021-02-16-traditional-courts-bill-rural-womens-access-to-justice-is-betrayed-again/.
51 Interview July 2012.
52 An individual claimant must exhaust all levels of the traditional court system before a matter can be referred to a Magistrate's court.
53 Hansard. Proceedings of the National Council of Provinces, Wednesday, December 02, 2020 [https://pmg.org.za/hansard/31783/].
54 In its concluding observations on the fourth periodic report of Botswana (2019), the CEDAW Committee reiterated its concern about the status of customary law and its recommendation that Botswana repeal Section 15, No. 4 of the Constitution.
55 Interview with a member of the women's movement, July 2012.
56 Ngwaketse customary law is the customary law of the Bangwaketse ethnic group, one of the largest ethnic groups found in the southern part of Botswana.

57 *Mmusi and Others v. Ramantele and Another* (MAHLB-000836–10), [2012] BWHC 1 (October 12, 2012, High Court) para 187.
58 *Ramantele v. Mmusi and Others*, September 3, 2013, Court of Appeal.
59 The Court of Appeal's decision set aside the reasoning in the High Court ruling by finding that customary law stood as a system of law, and as such, should be interpreted as flexible (Weinberg 2016, 198).
60 Act No. 116 of 1998 as amended by Act No. 14 of 2021: Domestic Violence Amendment Act, 2021. Available at: www.gov.za/sites/default/files/gcis_document/202203/45824gen788.pdf.
61 As amended by Act No. 13 of 2021: Criminal Law (Sexual Offences and Related Matters) Amendment Act, 2021. Available at: www.gov.za/sites/default/files/gcis_document/202203/45823gen787.pdf.
62 *Director of Public Prosecutions, Western Cape v Prins and Others* (369/12) [2012] ZASCA 106; 2012 (2) SACR 183 (SCA); 2012 (10) BCLR 1049 (SCA); [2012] 3 All SA 245 (SCA) (June 15, 2012).
63 Ibid, para 2 citing *S & another v Acting Regional Magistrate, Boksburg: Venter & another* (CCT 109/10) [2011] ZACC 22; 2011 (2) SACR 274 (CC) para 23.
64 *Levenstein and Others v Estate of the Late Sidney Lewis Frankel and Others* (CCT170/17) [2018] ZACC 16; 2018 (8) BCLR 921 (CC); 2018 (2) SACR 283 (CC) (June 14, 2018).
65 The Sexual Offences Amendment Act makes it a crime for a person to force another person to rape someone. This is known as compelled rape.
66 *S v Baloyi and Others* (CCT29/99) [1999] ZACC 19; 2000 (1) BCLR 86; 2000 (2) SA 425 (CC) (December 3, 1999).
67 *Carmichele v Minister of Safety and Security* (CCT 48/00) [2001] ZACC 22; 2001 (4) SA 938 (CC); 2001 (10) BCLR 995 (CC) (August 16, 2001).
68 *F v Minister of Safety and Security and Another* (CCT 30/11) [2011] ZACC 37; 2012 (1) SA 536 (CC); 2012 (3) BCLR 244 (CC); (2012) 33 ILJ 93 (CC); 2013 (2) SACR 20 (CC) (December 15, 2011). See Spies (2019) for a fuller discussion of the jurisprudence related to the police duty to protect.
69 Robin-Lee Francke, "Thousands protest in South Africa over rising violence against women" the *Guardian* (September 5, 2019). Available at: www.theguardian.com/world/2019/sep/05/thousands-protest-in-south-africa-over-rising-violence-against-women.
70 "President calls joint sitting of parliament on South Africa's changed approach to violence against women" Press Release of Parliament, Friday 13 September 2019 available at: www.parliament.gov.za/press-releases/president-calls-joint-sitting-parliament-south-africas-changed-approach-violence-against-women.
71 Criminal and Related Matters Amendment Act (No. 12, 2021); Sexual Offences and Related Matters Amendment Act (No. 13, 2021); Domestic Violence Amendment Act (No. 14, 2021).
72 Penal Code (Ch. 8:01) as amended by the Penal Code Amendment Act (No. 5 of 1998). The revised penal code set a minimum sentence for rape at 10 years, 15 years if the offender is HIV positive and 20 if the offender knew their HIV status before committing the offense (Thompson and Simmonds 2012).
73 In 2019, the High Court ruled that the provisions criminalizing same-sex conduct were found unconstitutional in *Letsweletse Motshidiemang v Attorney General*; LEGABIBO (Amicus Curiae) MAHGB- 000591–16., 6 (High Court. 2019).
74 In 2019, the Botswana Police Service Commissioner announced it would no longer allow cases to be withdrawn from the magistrate court docket. See the United States Department of State (2020) Botswana 2020 Human Rights Report available at: www.state.gov/wp-content/uploads/2021/03/BOTSWANA-2020-HUMAN-RIGHTS-REPORT.pdf (accessed June 12, 2022).

75 CEDAW (2019) List of issues and questions in relation to the fourth periodic report of Botswana. Addendum—Replies of Botswana to the list of issues and questions, (para 7. CEDAW/C/BWA/Q/4/Add.1 Available at OHCHR.org.

76 CEDAW (2019) Concluding observations on the fourth periodic report of Botswana, paragraph 25. CEDAW/C/BWA/CO/4. Available at OHCHR.org.

77 Botswana's sexual offenses laws are contained in the Penal Code Act 1964, as amended by the Penal Code (Amendment) Act 2005 (PC). The Criminal Procedure and Evidence Act 1939 (CPEA) contains the rules of evidence which apply to sexual assault offenses.

78 President Masisi, Statement on Gender Based Violence, September 18, 2020.

79 *S v Matlho* (CLCLB 019–07) [2008] BWCA 36 (January 1, 2008).

80 2020 UNAIDs reports the infection rate in Botswana for women aged 15–49 is 24.8% compared to 15.2% for men. For young women, the rate of infection (8.8%) is double that of young men (4.2%). In South Africa, infection rates are similar: 24.7% for women and 13.5% for men in the same age range. Among youth the rates are 10.4% and 3.5%, respectively.

81 Guttmacher Institute, South Africa country profile, 2022, www.guttmacher.org/geography/africa/south-africa; and Botswana country profile, 2022, www.guttmacher.org/geography/africa/botswana.

82 The Choice on Termination of Pregnancy Act provides for abortion on request within the first 12 weeks of pregnancy and between 13 and 20 weeks in consultation with a medical provider.

83 The 2004 Amendment (Act No. 38 of 2004), was declared invalid in the constitutional court case, *Doctors for Life International v Speaker of the National Assembly and others*, 2006 (6) SA416 CC because Parliament did not meet the constitutional obligation to facilitate public involvement before passing the bill. The 2008 Amendment (Act No. 1 of 2008) was subsequently passed.

84 Christian Lawyers Association of SA and Others v Minister of Health and Others 1998 (11) BCLR 1434 (T) Division: High Court, Transvaal Provincial Division Date: 10/07/1998 Case No: 16291/97.

85 Page 1443 of 1998 (11) BCLR 1434 (T)

86 *Christian Lawyers Association v The Minister of Health 2005* (1) SA 509 (T).

87 Private Members' Legislative Proposals and Special Petitions: Standing Committee. 7 September 2007 "Dudley's Constitution Seventeenth Amendment Bill: Introduction" available at: https://pmg.org.za/committee-meeting/10222/.

88 Choice on Termination of Pregnancy Amendment Bill—Ms. C Dudley (ACDP) (B34–2017) Available at https://pmg.org.za/bill/748/.

89 "Choice on Termination of Pregnancy Amendment Bill [B34–2017]: Bill rejected" Portfolio Committee on Health, Session May 9, 2018. Available at: https://pmg.org.za/committee-meeting/26316/.

90 If the pregnancy is a result of rape, incest, or defilement; if the woman is mentally deficient; if the woman's physical or mental health is at risk; or in cases of fetal abnormality.

91 For example, the most recent GenderLinks opinion survey reports that "only 43% respondents agreed or strongly agreed that a woman has the right to insist on a man using a condom." GenderLinks 2021 Gender Progress Score (GPS) Gender attitudes in Botswana Available at: https://genderlinks.org.za/wp-content/uploads/2021/08/BotswanaGPS_GenderAttitudes_Final_checked_mbfhmball_082021.pdf.

92 Affirmative action only applies to employers with 50 or more workers or a certain level of turnover.

93 *Lukie v Rural Alliance CC t/a Rural Developments Specialists* (2004) 25 ILJ 1445 (LC).

94 *De Beer v SA Export Connection CC t/a Golden Paws* (2008) 29 ILJ 347 (LC).

95 *Woolworths (Pty) Ltd v Whitehead* (CA06/99) [2000] ZALAC 4 (April 3, 2000).

96 Introduction of the "Code of Good Practice on the Handling of Sexual Harassment Cases in the Workplace" as amended and published 2005 in the Government Gazette Available at: //www.gov.za/sites/default/files/gcis_document/201409/278650.pdf.

97 *Ntsabo v Real Security* CC 2003 24 ILJ 2341 (LC) is a landmark case concerning employer liability for sexual harassment.
98 *Moatswi v Fencing Centre (Pty)* 2002 1 BLR 262 (IC).
99 *David v Auto & General Supplies* 2007 3 BLR 265 (IC).
100 Art 9(2) Maternity Protection Convention.
101 Botswana is not a signatory to ILO 190, the Convention on Sexual Harassment in the Workplace.
102 Section 38 of the PSA provides: "(1) . . . Sexual harassment of one employee by another, or by a person in authority over another in the public service, shall constitute misconduct."
103 Interview with a former member of parliament and member of the women's movement, July 2012.

References

Albertyn, Catherine. 2005. "Defending and Securing Rights Through Law: Feminism, Law and The Courts in South Africa." *Politikon* 32, no. 2: 217–237. DOI: 10.1080/02589340500353474.

Albertyn, Catherine. 2019a. "Abortion, Reproductive Rights and the Possibilities of Reproductive Justice in South African Courts." *University of Oxford Human Rights Hub Journal* 1: 87–119.

Albertyn, Catherine. 2019b. "(In)equality and the South African Constitution." *Development Southern Africa* 36, no. 6: 751–766. DOI: 10.1080/0376835X.2019.1660860.

Alexander, Elsie M., ed. 2005. *Beyond Inequalities 2005: Women in Botswana*. Zimbabwe: Southern African Research & Documentation Centre (SARDC).

Andrews, Penelope E. 1998. "Striking the Rock: Confronting Gender Equality in South Africa." *Michigan Journal of Race and Law* 3, no. 2 (Spring): 307–339.

Bauer, Gretchen and Scott D. Taylor. 2005. *Politics in Southern Africa: State and Society in Transition*. Boulder: Lynne Reinner.

Berro Pizzarossa, Lucía and Ebenezer Durojaye. 2019. "International Human Rights Norms and The South African Choice on Termination of Pregnancy Act: An Argument for Vigilance And Modernisation." *South African Journal on Human Rights* 35, no. 1: 50–69. DOI: 10.1080/02587203.2019.1589388.

Britton, Hannah E. 2002. "Coalition Building, Election Rules, and Party Politics: South African Women's Path to Parliament." *Africa Today* 49, no. 4: 33–67.

Britton, Hannah E. 2020. *Ending Gender-Based Violence: Justice and Community in South Africa*. Urbana: University of Illinois Press.

Claassens, Aninka. 2009. "Who Told Them We Want This Bill? The Traditional Courts Bill and Rural Women." *Agenda: Empowering Women for Gender Equity* 2009, no. 82: 9–22. www.jstor.org/stable/41321364.

Dinokopila, Bonolo Ramadi and Bonno Kgoboge. 2021. "Customary Law and Limitations to Constitutional Rights in Botswana." *Nordic Journal of Human Rights* 39, no. 3: 339–357. DOI: 10.1080/18918131.2021.1986289.

Fombad, Charles Manga. 2004. "The Constitutional Protection against Discrimination in Botswana." *International and Comparative Law Quarterly* 53: 139–170.

Geisler, Gisela. 2004. *Women and the Remaking of Politics in Southern Africa*. Uppsala: Nordiska Afrikainstitutet.

Gouws, Amanda. 2004. "The Politics of State Structures: Citizenship and the National Machinery for Women in South Africa." *Feminist Africa* 3: 1–12.

Gouws, Amanda and Hayley Galgut. 2016. "Twenty Years of the Constitution: Reflecting on Citizenship and Gender Justice." *Agenda* 30, no.1: 3–9. DOI: 10.1080/10130950.2016.1204818.

Gouws, Amanda and Diana Højlund Madsen. 2021. "Beijing +25." *Agenda* 35 no. 2: 3–17. DOI: 10.1080/10130950.2021.1930894.

Guttmacher Institute. 2017. "Abortion Worldwide 2017: Uneven Progress and Unequal Access." [online] Available at: www.guttmacher.org/sites/default/files/report_pdf/abortion-worldwide-2017.pdf.

Guttmacher, Sally, Farzana Kapadia, Jim Te Water Naude, and Helen de Pinho. 1998. "Abortion Reform in South Africa: A Case Study of the 1996 Choice on Termination of Pregnancy Act." *International Family Planning Perspectives* 24, no. 4: 191–194. DOI: 10.2307/2991980.

Hassim, Shireen. 2002. "A Conspiracy of Women: The Women's Movement in South Africa's Transition to Democracy." *Social Research* 69, no. 3: 603–630.

Himsworth, C. M. G. 1974. "Effects of Matrimonial Causes Legislation in Botswana." *Journal of African Law* 18, no. 2: 173–179.

Human Rights Council (HRC) of the United Nations. 2016. Report of the Special Rapporteur on violence against women, its causes, and consequences on her mission to South Africa. 14 June 2016. A/HRC/32/42/Add.2 Available at: www.refworld.org/docid/57d90a4b4.html.

Hunter, Chris. 2006. "The Master's Tools Revisited: Can Law Contribute to Ending Violence Against Women?" *Institute Development Studies Bulletin* 37, no. 6: 57–68. https://doi.org/10.1111/j.1759-5436.2006.tb00323.x.

International Commission of Jurists (ICJ). 2013. "Women's Access to Justice in Botswana: Identifying the Obstacles and Need for Change." Geneva Switzerland [ISBN: 92-9037-159-5].

Jonas, Obonye. 2013. "Gender Equality in Botswana: The Case of Mmusi and Others v Ramantele and Others." *African Human Rights Law Journal* 13, no. 1: 229–244.

Kalabamu, Faustin Tirwirukwa. 2006. "Patriarchy and Women's Land Rights in Botswana." *Land Use Policy* 23, no. 3(July): 237–246. DOI: 10.1016/j.landusepol.2004.11.001.

Kalabamu, Faustin Tirwirukwa. 2021. "A commentary on Botswana's 2019 National Land Policy." *Land Use Policy* 108 (September): 105563. DOI: 10.1016/j.landusepol.2021.105563.

Lambert, Priscilla A. and Druscilla L. Scribner. 2020. "Constitutions and Women's Rights Advocacy: Strategic Uses of Gender Provisions in Argentina, Chile, Botswana, and South Africa." *Politics, Groups, and Identities* 8, no. 2: 228–247. DOI: 10.1080/21565503.2018.1449759.

Leslie, Agnes Ngoma. 2006. *Social Movements and Democracy in Africa: The Impact of Women's Struggle for Equal Rights in Botswana*. New York: Routledge.

Machisa, Mercy and Roos van Dorp. 2012. "Gender-Based Violence Indicators Study. Gaborone: Gender Links and Ministry of Labour and Home Affairs, Women's Affairs Department." Available at: http://genderlinks.org.za/wp-content/uploads/imported/articles/attachments/15554_gbv_indicators_executivesummary.pdf.

Mogapaesi, Tshepo. 2019. "Sexual Harassment in the Workplace and Women's Access to Justice: Lessons for Botswana From a South African Perspective." *Commonwealth Law Bulletin* 45, no. 3: 431–453. DOI: 10.1080/03050718.2020.1737552.

Mogapaesi, Tshepo. 2022. "An Overview of Maternity Protection in Botswana: A Critique of the Employment Act Through the International Labour Organisation's Maternity Protection Convention Lens." *De Jure Law Journal* 55, no. 1: 57–76. https://dx.doi.org/10.17159/2225-7160/2022/v55a4.

Mogobe, Keitshokile Dintle, Wananani Tshiamo, and Motsholathebe Bowelo. 2007. "Monitoring Maternal Mortality in Botswana." *Reproductive Health Matters* 15, no. 30: 163–171. DOI: 10.1016/S0968–8080(07)30330–3.

Mogwe, Alice. 1992. "Botswana: Abortion 'Debate' Dynamics." *Agenda: Empowering Women for Gender Equity* 1992, no. 12: 41–43. https://doi.org/10.2307/4065475.

Molokomme, Athaliah. 1991. "Emang Basadi." *Signs: Journal of Women in Culture and Society* 6, no. 4: 848–851.

Ngwako, Karabo and Aduragbemi Banke-Thomas. 2020. " 'I guess we have to Treat them, but . . . ': Health Care Provider Perspectives on Management of Women Presenting with Unsafe Abortion in Botswana." *Global Public Health* 15, no. 9: 1308–1321. DOI: 10.1080/17441692.2020.1751863.

Nkhwalume, Ludo and Yohana Mashalla. 2019. "Maternal Mortality Trends at the Princess Marina and Nyangabwe Referral Hospitals in Botswana." *African Health Sciences* 19, no. 2: 1833–1840. DOI: 10.4314/ahs.v19i2.5.

Osman, Fatima. 2018. "Third Time a Charm? The Traditional Courts Bill 2017." *South African Crime Quarterly*, no. 64: 45–53. https://dx.doi.org/10.17159/2413-3108/2018/v0n64a4870.

O'Sullivan, Michelle and Christina Murray. 2005. "Brooms Sweeping Oceans? Women's Rights in South Africa's First Decade of Democracy." *Acta Juridica* 17: 1–41.

Phaladze, Nthabiseng and Sheila Tlou. 2006. "Gender and HIV/AIDS in Botswana: A Focus on Inequalities and Discrimination." *Gender & Development* 14, no. 1: 23–35. DOI: 10.1080/13552070500518095.

Pickles, Camilla. 2012. "Termination-of-Pregnancy Rights and Foetal Interests in Continued Existence in South Africa: The Choice on Termination of Pregnancy Act 92 of 1996." *Potchefstroom Electronic Law Journal* 15, no. 5: 403–434. DOI: 10.4314/pelj.v15i5.11.

Quansah, E. K. 2005. "Abolition of Marital Power in Botswana: A New Dimension in Marital Relationship?" *University of Botswana Law Journal* 1, no 6 (June 2005): 5–27. DOI: 10.10520/AJA18172733_179.

Scribner, Druscilla, and Priscilla A. Lambert. 2010. "Constitutionalizing Difference: A Case Study Analysis of Gender Provisions in Botswana and South Africa." *Politics & Gender* 6, no. 1: 37–61. DOI: 10.1017/S1743923X0999050X.

Sechele, Unaludo. 2022. "From Minors to Equals? Kalanga Women and Marriage Legislation in Post-Colonial Botswana, 1966–2005." *Historia* 67, no. 1: 114–143. https://dx.doi.org/10.17159/2309-8392/2021/v67n1a5

Seidman, Gay W. 1999. "Gendered Citizenship: South Africa's Democratic Transition and the Construction of a Gendered State." *Gender and Society* 13, no. 3: 287–307.

Selolwane, O. D. 1998. "Equality of Citizenship and the Gendering of Democracy in Botswana." In *Botswana, Politics and Society*, edited by W. A. Edge and M. H. Lekorwe. Pretoria: J. L. Schaik.

Spies, Amanda. 2019. "Continued State Liability for Police Inaction in Assisting Victims of Domestic Violence: A Reflection on the Implementation of South Africa's Domestic Violence Legislation." *Journal of African Law* 63, no. 1: 53–77. DOI: 10.1017/S0021855319000081.

Smith, Stephanie Samantha. 2013. "The Challenges Procuring of Safe Abortion Care in Botswana." *African Journal of Reproductive Health/La Revue Africaine de la Santé Reproductive* 17, no. 4: 43–55.

Tabengwa, Monica, and Nancy Nicol. 2013. "The Development of Sexual Rights and the LGBT Movement in Botswana." In *Human Rights, Sexual Orientation and Gender Identity in The Commonwealth*, edited by Corinne Lennox and Matthew Waites, 339–358. London: University of London Press.

Thipe, Thuto. 2013. *Voices in the Legislative Process: A Report on the Public Submissions on the Traditional Courts Bill (2008 and 2012)*. University of Cape Town, Faculty of Law, Centre for Law and Society, 2013. Available at: http://hdl.handle.net/11427/2462.

Thompson, Jill and Felly Nkewto Simmonds. 2012. Rape Sentencing Study: A Review of Statutory Sentencing Provisions for Rape, Defilement, and Sexual Assault in East, Central, and Southern Africa. Lusaka: Population Council. Available at: https://knowledgecommons.popcouncil.org/departments_sbsr-rh/12/

Tripp, Aili Mari. 2004. "Women's Movements, Customary Law, and Land Rights in Africa: The Case of Uganda." *African Studies Quarterly* 7, no. 4: 1–19.

Usdin, Shereen, Nicola Christofides, Lebo Malepe and Aadielah Maker. 2000. "The Value of Advocacy in Promoting Social Change: Implementing the New Domestic Violence Act in South Africa." *Reproductive Health Matters* 8, no. 16: 55–65. DOI: 10.1016/S0968–8080(00)90187–3

Van Allen, Judith. 2000. "'Bad Future Things' and Liberatory Moments: Capitalism and the State in Botswana." *Radical History Review* 2000, no. 76: 136–168.

Van Allen, Judith. 2007. "Feminism and Social Democracy in Botswana." *Socialism and Democracy* 21, no. 3: 97–126.

Waylen, Georgina. 2007a. "Women's Mobilization and Gender Outcomes in Transitions to Democracy: The Case of South Africa." *Comparative Political Studies* 40, no. 5: 521–546.

Waylen, Georgina. 2007b. *Engendering Transitions: Women's Mobilization, Institutions, and Gender Outcomes*. Oxford, New York: Oxford University Press.

Weeks, Sindiso Mnisi. 2011. "Beyond the Traditional Courts Bill: Regulating Customary Courts in Line With Living Customary Law and the Constitution." *South African Crime Quarterly* 2011, no. 35: 31–40. DOI: 10.17159/2413–3108/2011/v0i35a870.

Women's Legal Centre (LRC). 2010. "Sexual Harassment" and the amended Code of Good Practice on the Handling of Sexual Harassment in South Africa." Published by the Women's Legal Centre originally in 2006, republished in 2010. Available at: https://shukumisa.org.za/wp-content/uploads/2017/09/Sexual-Harassment-English.pdf.

Weinberg, Tara. 2016 "Pushing the Boundaries of Customary Law Jurisprudence in Botswana: Social Science and the Law in the Case of Ramantele vs. Mmusi." *The Journal of Legal Pluralism and Unofficial Law* 48, no. 2: 186–207. DOI: 10.1080/07329113.2016.1169056.

Williams, Susan. 2009. *Constituting Equality: Gender Equality and Comparative Constitutional Law*, edited by Susan Williams. Cambridge: Cambridge University Press.

6

CONCLUSION

Priscilla A. Lambert and Druscilla L. Scribner

> So if you asked me whether, in general, it was best to have a neutral constitution, I would tend to say, no. Because . . . constitutions are not made for a single period, they must endure through historical, economic, and social transformation. Where there is gender discrimination, a neutral constitution will not work to make it visible.
>
> —*Lawyer and Legal Advocate, Chile, Interview 2011*

Introduction

Nearly every country around the world now recognizes women's equality in its constitution. Some constitutions do so minimally, while others obligate the state to take proactive measures to redress gender inequality and promote women's full participation in society. Still, others constitutionalize women's traditional caregiving and reproductive roles and require that the state protect women as mothers. Whether or not these different constitutional provisions matter for women's equality is the question that originally motivated this research. Based on the assumption that institutions such as the national constitution construct gender power and play a role in reproducing gender inequality, we wanted to examine how different conceptualizations of gender equality can be used to challenge and reshape the status quo.

The question is embedded in a larger literature about the relationship between the law and social change. The law structures power relationships and defines a political and social community. It creates, recreates, or challenges gendered power asymmetries and marginalization. It is not surprising, then, that women have sought to shape constitutions in ways that are inclusive and accommodating of women, that recognize equal status for women, and/or that seek to dismantle

DOI: 10.4324/9781003303725-6

structural sources of gender-based discrimination. Constitutional gender provisions have transformative potential that is mediated by social and political forces. This study has systematically categorized how women's equality and social roles are recognized in constitutions and examined how different constitutional provisions provide legal tools that create or constrain opportunities for social and political actors to achieve change.

In the previous chapters, we presented a comprehensive comparative study of gender equality in national constitutions that includes a quantitative cross-national study focused on broad equality outcomes and qualitative case studies focused on process—how constitutional provisions aid or hinder rights advocates' efforts to press for or defend women-friendly policy change through legislatures and courts—and on legislative and judicial outcomes. The results paint a complex picture. Social transformation for women and people with other marginalized identities intersecting with gender is often frustrated, unrealized, partial, and disappointingly slow. Yet change is taking place. Overall, the gaps between men and women are narrowing in every policy area.

The two regional case studies demonstrate that where constitutional provisions for gender equality are substantive and egalitarian, as in South Africa and Argentina, these provisions are central to civil society actors' work in policy advocacy and legal mobilization. In Botswana and Chile, the absence of egalitarian provisions has encouraged advocates to reach around the national constitution and rely on international law to legitimate their claims and provide weapons in the fight for favorable policies and court decisions. Despite the stubborn gaps between rights and reality for women, the transformative potential of law is attractive to feminists. Since we began this study, the movement to incorporate gender and substantive rights into the constitution has gained ground. It now looms large in public debates about constitutional reform in Chile and Botswana.

Constitutional Provisions and Gender Equality Gaps

We began our study by systematically coding for gender rights and provisions in national constitutions from 1995 to 2015. Our database now includes every provision that mentions gender, sex, motherhood, and family in over 100 countries at three points in time. We also code for whether these are formal rights that seek to remove legal barriers (gender-neutral), whether they recognize gender difference but primarily on the basis of women's reproductive and caregiving roles (maternal), or whether they are substantive rights that obligate the state to take steps to redress sex discrimination and actively promote women's equality (egalitarian). These distinctions are important because we expected that egalitarian provisions would be the most likely to challenge structures that subordinate women to men. In contrast, neutral and maternal provisions set men as the baseline or reinforce women's traditional roles and are less likely to promote true equality.

We drew upon our database of national constitutions to test whether the presence of egalitarian or maternal provisions is positively associated with outcomes that measure legal guarantees and protections and with global measures of women's equality. The cross-national results suggest that egalitarian gender provisions are associated with legal frameworks that protect women and/or promote women's equality. These simple comparisons do not, however, control for other factors. We also used the World Economic Forum's Gender Gap Index to test whether the presence of egalitarian provisions and maternal provisions has an effect on women's equality in a multivariate analysis. We also used Gender Gap subindices that measure women's economic, political, and health outcomes relative to men as measures of the dependent variable. The panel data analysis reveals that egalitarian provisions are positively associated with better outcomes for women, while maternal provisions are negatively associated with measures of women's equality. This finding holds even though constitutional gender provisions are most commonly found in some of the poorest and least developed countries where women's status is low, and countries with few or no gender provisions are concentrated in the most developed countries where women enjoy significantly more rights protected by statute.

Process and Outcomes—Comparing Across Regions

The fight for justice is "done on four legs," one of our Argentine interviewees remarked, explaining the relationship between litigation, mobilization, media coverage, and legislation. In the case studies, we explored how constitutional provisions aid or hinder advocacy efforts associated with two of these legs—legislation and litigation. Having compared neighboring countries with and without egalitarian provisions, we conclude with a cross-regional comparison and explore the similarities in process and outcomes for South Africa and Argentina in contrast to Chile and Botswana.

Legislating

The presence or absence of gender provisions can facilitate or thwart efforts to secure legislative change, whether through lobbying by advocacy groups or in legislative committees and on the floor of national assemblies. In each comparative case study, we examined how constitutional provisions supporting gender equality or, alternatively, supporting a maternal role and protections for women or families affect these legislative efforts. In South Africa and Argentina, egalitarian provisions lent legitimacy to rights-based argumentation, enabled efforts to reform policy, and were associated with more women-friendly judicial outcomes. Our interviewees readily agreed that constitutional provisions were a tool for advocacy—one among several that could be leveraged in their work. Meanwhile, in Chile and Botswana, debates and legislation are far less likely to refer to the constitution or women's rights, and often the laws that are passed are more limited in scope.

Regardless of their position within or outside the state, interviewees in Argentina and South Africa described their constitutions as egalitarian and transformative. Individual activists revealed a myriad of activities that were made possible by gender provisions: to set the agenda, to educate (legislators, judges, and the public) and raise awareness, to justify laws in parliamentary debates, and to block discriminatory laws.

The laws and debates in Argentina and South Africa regularly cited constitutional rights and incorporated egalitarian provisions into the legislation. In both countries, interviewees reported that key pieces of legislation would not have been possible without the rights enumerated in the constitution. Egalitarian provisions, they said, lent legitimacy to arguments that otherwise would have been "very arduous" to make. This legitimacy was especially important as they sought to persuade conservative colleagues and counter deeply rooted stereotypes in conservative provinces. Importantly, egalitarian rights in both constitutions obligate the state to act. These obligations have made their way into laws and strengthened them. For example, reproductive health legislation in Argentina specifies that the state must provide and fund contraception services because of guarantees in international treaties that have constitutional status.

Egalitarian provisions also clarify what is not legitimate and provide a critical backstop to protect hard-won rights and laws. In South Africa, advocates explained that the Constitution sets the baseline and that all laws begin with the question of whether they will pass constitutional muster. As noted in Chapter 5, a private bill seeking to regulate abortion clinics was "stopped in its tracks" when experts testified that it was unconstitutional. Thus, constitutional rights and discourse are deployed to prevent the erosion of women's rights.

In contrast, Chile and Botswana take a neutral approach to gender in their constitutions. Interviewees in both countries emphasized that gender neutrality masks a male bias and perpetuates patriarchy. Although the equality statements in both countries are not viewed as transformative, they lend legitimacy to efforts to repeal or prevent explicitly discriminatory laws. However, there was no evidence that sex equality provisions were used to pass proactive measures to increase women's political or economic power. In fact, some attempts to enact positive discrimination policies were rejected as violating the right to equality.

In both countries, key provisions entrenching tradition and gender stereotypes undermined women's rights and provided legitimacy for arguments by opponents of gender equality. In Chile, the constitutional protection of the family has been effectively used by the political right to block or minimize gender policy. In committee and floor debates, a discourse on family and women as mothers held more sway than arguments based on women's rights. Thus, legislation was reframed in terms of women's traditional caregiving role and constitutional protection of the family to secure its passage. Likewise, the constitutional status of customary law is an enormous obstacle to women claiming equal rights in Botswana, as detailed in Chapter 5.

Given this less favorable domestic legal environment, international law takes on greater importance. In the absence of egalitarian provisions, combined with the presence of provisions that may run counter to women's rights, advocates in both countries reported that they rely more heavily on international law. In both countries, advocates identified CEDAW and the CEDAW Committee reporting and monitoring process as especially useful for legitimating their claims, advancing legal reform, and sanctioning the state when it is not meeting its international obligations.

Across the four country cases, the constitutional status of international law and the domestic use of international norms in advocacy efforts are noteworthy. In Argentina, the legal hierarchy is clear: international treaties such as CEDAW have constitutional status. Advocates view international and regional conventions and human rights standards as having a significant and positive effect when the language of these instruments is directly incorporated into domestic law. In South Africa, advocates indicated that while international and regional legal instruments were helpful, the Constitution provides ample tools to advocate for policy change and to hold the state accountable for policy implementation failures. In Chile and Botswana, by contrast, advocates seemed to draw upon international law as a second-best strategy. The absence of clearly enumerated rights for women in their national constitutions increases the reliance upon international laws and treaties. At the same time, the uncertain status of international law in the domestic legal hierarchy significantly limits its usefulness in Chile and Botswana.

Litigating

The way gender equality is constitutionalized is an important part of the legal opportunity structure for women's rights organizations. In each case study, we examined whether egalitarian provisions affect the decision to turn to the courts and reported the case-level outcomes when they did. The case studies indicate that advocates are more likely to pursue a litigation strategy in South Africa and Argentina and less likely to do so in Chile and Botswana. The case studies also show that the presence of egalitarian provisions in the constitution mattered for winning women's rights cases, raising awareness and mobilizing people, and providing judges with the latitude to develop the law.

Legal advocacy organizations are well-developed and professionalized in South Africa and Argentina. These organizations are working to increase awareness of women's rights, provide rights-based arguments, monitor policy implementation, document violations, file amicus curiae or third-party briefs, and represent clients. In South Africa, those involved in litigation highlighted the importance of egalitarian provisions for providing legitimacy for rights claims. Gender equality, they contended, is "a very big card to put on the table" in court.

Those involved in litigation noted that the presence of constitutional rights affected their strategies and that they often use constitutional provisions to help raise media awareness and put issues on the agenda. For example, some organizations pursue a litigation strategy even when a win is unlikely to highlight the state's failure to act or meet its constitutional obligations to ensure individual rights are implemented.

Egalitarian provisions that obligate the state to act can play an important role in judicial outcomes. In South Africa, for example, the courts have frequently ruled that constitutional rights to freedom from violence and rights to bodily and psychological integrity mean the state has a positive duty to protect women in cases concerning violence against women. In Argentina, substantive rights to equality of opportunity in the Constitution have been cited in court decisions that imposed proactive measures on private employers.

Legal mobilization is not as well developed in Chile and Botswana. In both countries, few constitutional claims to women's rights or equality are made in the courts. Nonetheless, in Botswana, constitutional challenges on the grounds of gender discrimination, for example, concerning citizenship and inheritance rights, have been influential. At the same time, the constitutional status of customary law is an obstacle to the practical ability of women to claim their individual rights. In Chile, when women do litigate, they use the statute, rather than the Constitution, as the starting point. In the vast majority of discrimination cases, women do not make constitutional rights claims. In both countries, the lawyers and advocates we interviewed suggested that women's rights arguments were not a "winning strategy" in court.

The absence of egalitarian provisions has also meant that judges, including progressive judges, have less latitude when handing down decisions regarding women's rights. This dynamic is apparent in Botswana, where the constitutional position of customary law vis-à-vis women's rights puts significant pressure on the High Court and the Court of Appeals. If the court upholds gender equality rights by reading international obligations, it is open to criticism for reaching beyond its legitimate role. In contrast, lawyers and judges in Argentina, and even more so in South Africa, regularly reference rights to equality in the constitution and international law in their decisions without fear of criticism for overstepping their role or harming judicial legitimacy.

In all four countries, rights advocates engaged in legal mobilization and litigation draw upon international law to make rights claims. In Argentina and South Africa, such arguments are viewed as legitimate and are part of the jurisprudence; in Chile and Botswana, international law arguments are viewed with skepticism but are often the only basis for rights claims. In these countries, international law can be an unpredictable tool.

Connecting Qualitative and Quantitative Results

The advantage of using a mixed methods approach is that it helps avoid some of the pitfalls associated with using only quantitative or qualitative methods. While quantitative methods allow the researcher to control for many factors in the policy-making process, the effects of law on society are best assessed with in-depth case study analyses that allow the researcher to gain detailed knowledge that may yield new and valuable insights. When both quantitative and qualitative results are consistent, as ours are, we can be more confident in concluding that constitutional provisions matter.

The quantitative analysis tracked equality outcomes and constitutional provisions over time and across countries and found that egalitarian rights matter for women's equality outcomes, while maternal provisions have a negative impact. Our case studies show that women's rights advocates fight to have egalitarian rights included in their constitutions and regularly use them in their advocacy efforts in the legislature and the courts. These rights then affect processes and outcomes: they provide the foundation for advocates' arguments and help them raise awareness. They have played a role in getting more progressive or women-friendly legislation and judicial decisions in Argentina and South Africa. Also, they have been used to prevent policy reversal and support efforts to hold the government accountable for implementing existing legislation.

The literature on the effect of constitutional provisions has tended to arrive at different results depending on the method of analysis: qualitative studies tend to be more optimistic than quantitative studies about the effects of constitutional provisions. Our quantitative and qualitative results, however, are consistent and reinforce each other. One reason our quantitative and qualitative analyses arrive at similar results may be because we are able to include a theoretically important variable that is often missing in large N statistical analyses—mobilization. Although the feminist mobilization variable did not behave as expected in our statistical models, existing qualitative studies and this one indicate that mobilization of citizen groups or NGOs is a key variable and likely interacts with other explanatory variables in important ways. Going forward, quantitative analyses of the effects of constitutions should find ways to incorporate this critical variable or risk biased results.

Another reason may be that in both our qualitative and quantitative analyses, we distinguish between different types of provisions and recognize that not all gender rights are promoting equality. Our comparative case studies revealed that political actors on both sides of an issue use constitutional provisions in their attempts to influence laws and policy. Thus, the presence of a right to equality may be trumped by cultural rights in the constitution, as in Botswana, or by the state's obligation to protect the family, as we saw in Chile in Chapter 4. In other words, constitutional rights may conflict with or cancel each other out. By separating out egalitarian and maternal provisions and including customary law provisions, we capture important differences and contradictions in constitutions that have not been included in other quantitative studies.

Constitutional Reform Efforts in Chile and Botswana

In September 2022, Chileans went to the polls to vote on the draft constitution. The draft was written by a constitutional assembly noted for its equal representation of women and men in a year-long process that followed several years of intense social protests. It included provisions on women's equality, indigenous rights protection, and social guarantees as well as a decentralization of power crafted to support a transformation toward a more egalitarian society. The provisions for women's equality were far-reaching and promoted substantive equality through an explicit gender equality statement and recognition of measures needed to overcome disadvantages, the right to be free from gender-based violence with an obligation for the state to act with due diligence to prevent and protect, and sexual and reproductive health rights focused on autonomy. It also guaranteed gender parity in the electoral system, public organizations, and the judiciary. There were several other egalitarian provisions that required the state to address gender-based rural inequality and violence, ensured labor rights including equal pay for equal work, and a right to comprehensive care and public policies that promote and incorporate human rights, gender, and intersectionality. In short, it was a very progressive document and Chilean voters rejected it overwhelmingly.[1]

In Botswana as well, rights advocates are seeking constitutional changes. A constitutional revision process in Botswana has its roots in a 2019 campaign promise by President Masisi. A Presidential Commission of Inquiry (the Dibotelo Commission) was appointed in late 2021 and began its work in 2022 to gather people's views on the constitution's strengths and weaknesses; assess how well it reflects identity, principles, aspirations, and values; and evaluate how well it promotes and protects rights, equality, and national unity and democracy. The Dibotelo Commission made recommendations to the President at the end of September 2022 regarding amendments and review[2]. Women had lobbied for and succeeded in gaining nearly equal representation on the Commission, and the public consultation process has opened the door for women's groups to identify weaknesses and suggest potential revisions that support gender equality.

Representatives of all five political parties and seven women's organizations in Botswana submitted a formal joint statement to the Commission of Inquiry in June 2022.[3] The submission drew on constitutions in the region and beyond, as well as on CEDAW Committee recommendations, and outlined key constitutional revisions that would recognize gender in a more egalitarian manner. The submission identified the formal approach to equality as problematic and limited and advocated for a substantive approach. This approach would be reflected in a revised gender equality statement that recognizes that women and men are equal, includes intersectional discrimination, and expands the grounds for non-discrimination beyond sex to include gender identity, sexual orientation, marital status, parental status, and pregnancy.

The group also recommended several standalone gender provisions that name and promote rights and freedoms for women explicitly, as well as the domestication of international law on gender and human rights. These provisions, they argued, would serve as legal and policy mechanisms to hold the government and the state accountable. The recommended gender provisions included a stipulation that customary law must comply with non-discrimination guarantees, recognition of international human rights law, affirmative action, and gender quotas, as well as rights that address gender-based violence, sexual and reproductive health, citizenship, and equality in marriage. The Commission recommended the adoption of a 30 percent candidate quotas in primary, local, and parliamentary elections and that termination of pregnancy be legalized. It did not recommend changes regarding the status of customary law.

The constitutional reforms proposed or recommended in Chile and Botswana include concrete provisions that would move their constitutions from a gender-neutral or a formal equality approach to a substantive equality approach that is largely egalitarian. Such changes have the potential to transform the position of women in these societies. Realizing that potential requires that the new rights be mobilized by social and political actors and used to support efforts to reform laws and practices. They must also be used to hold the state accountable for the implementation and enforcement of existing laws. The experiences of Argentina and South Africa highlight the opportunities and challenges that come with substantive egalitarian gender provisions.

Lessons for Women's Rights Advocacy

When we first began studying gender provisions over a decade ago, there was cause for optimism as women were making significant gains in terms of education, economic opportunity, and political representation. But over the last several years, there has been backlash and erosion of women's rights even in advanced democracies like the United States. As Amnesty International documents, women's rights are under attack and there have been serious reversals for women seeking to live free from violence, have control over their reproductive health, and enjoy economic security. Nationalist and populist movements, as well as right-wing political groups, have been at the forefront of these attacks. These trends have only been exacerbated by the COVID-19 pandemic, which has set women back about two decades in terms of economic equality and opportunity and has been accompanied by a dramatic increase in domestic violence.[4]

While constitutional provisions are not a guarantee, they are a strong barrier to conservative forces that seek to reverse the gains that women have won after decades of activism. Our research suggests that it is far more difficult to take away rights when they are constitutionalized. For example, in 2022 the U.S. Supreme Court overturned the landmark *Roe v. Wade* decision that had guaranteed women a right to abortion. In doing so, the Supreme Court majority ruled there was no constitutional right to abortion. The decision, *Dobbs v. Jackson Women's Health Organization*, upset 50 years of legal precedent and marked the first time that the US Supreme Court took away what was long considered a fundamental right. In response to a media question about the reversal of abortion rights in the United States, Cathi Albertyn, a law professor at the University of the Witwatersrand, summarized the protections for both privacy and reproductive rights in the South African Constitution and stated, "We have the kind of abortion law that American feminists dream of. And the chances of these [constitutional] protections changing are very slim."[5] Overall, the global trend to include more egalitarian gender provisions is a positive one for women's equality and preferable to fewer or no enumerated rights.

Notes

1 Despite 80% voting in favor of a new constitution just two years earlier, analysts believe that several factors contributed to its failure: low support for Chile's new President Boric who strongly supported the draft constitution, media campaigns making false claims about the draft, and a perception that the draft was too radical. President Boric has promised to start a new constitutional process. See, for example, Patricio Fernández, "The Rechazo—Why Chileans Rejected a New Constitution: An insider's account by a member of the Chilean Constitutional Convention." *The Nation,* September 26, 2022. Available at: www.thenation.com/article/world/rechazo-chile-rejection-new-constitution/. See also Vanessa Buschschlüter, "Chile Constitution: Voters Overwhelmingly Reject Radical Change." *BBC,* October 5, 2022. Available at: www.bbc.com/news/world-latin-america-62792025 www.thenation.com/article/world/rechazo-chile-rejection-new-constitution/.

2 The Commission recommended the adoption of a 30 percent candidate quotas in primary, local, and parliamentary elections and that termination of pregnancy be legalized. It did not recommend changes regarding the status of customary law. See p. 216 of the Final Report of the Presidential Commission of Inquiry 2022. The Report is available at: https://constitutionnet.org/sites/default/files/2022-12/Final%20Commission%20Report%2028%20Sep%202022.pdf.

3 *Submission to the Commission of Inquiry into the Review of the Constitution of Botswana* (the Dibotelo Commission) available at: https://genderlinks.org.za/wp-content/uploads/2022/06/BotswanaConstitutionSubmissionGender_062022.pdf.

4 "International Women's Day: Dramatic Deterioration in Respect for Women's Rights and Gender Equality must be Decisively Reversed." *Amnesty International,* March 7, 2022 Available at: www.amnesty.org/en/latest/news/2022/03/international-womens-day-dramatic-deterioration-in-respect-for-womens-rights-and-gender-equality-must-be-decisively-reversed/.

5 "Here's what will Happen in South Africa if the US Reverses Abortion Rights." *Mail and Guardian*, May 9, 2022. Available at: https://mg.co.za/health/2022-05-09-heres-what-will-happen-in-south-africa-if-the-us-reverses-abortion-rights/.

APPENDIX A

Coding Constitutions and Construction of Egalitarian and Maternal Provisions Scores

The database codes for 24 types of provisions at three points in time: 1995, 2005, and 2015. For consistency of translation, we relied almost entirely on two sources for national constitutions: *Constitutions of the Countries of the World* (subscription service)[1] and the Constitution Project's *Constitute Database*.[2] Each constitution was double-coded and then reconciled to produce a single cross-national database of gender provisions over 20 years. The UN Women's Global Gender Equality Constitutional Database[3] served as an additional reference when reconciling coding differences.

The constitutions are scored progressively such that provisions that obligate the state to act to remove barriers to gender equality receive higher scores. For example, in the area of sex discrimination, the coding method distinguishes between the presence of a simple non-discrimination statement on the basis of sex, the constitutionality of positive measures to overcome past discrimination, and the obligation of the state to pursue those kinds of measures and level the playing field for women.

In the following, we provide the coding rubric for all 24 provisions by category: general, political, social, and economic rights and provisions.

Coding Rubric

General Provisions

Equality:

(−1) Male language (e.g., "all men are equal")
(0) No gender or sex equality statement (all persons are equal)

(1) Sex equality statement (sex as one of many categories) or explicit statement about equality (e.g., "men and women are equal")

Non-Discrimination:

(0) No gender- or sex-specific non-discrimination statement
(1) Specific gender or sex non-discrimination statement
(2) Positive discrimination is constitutional or state obligation to overcome past gender-based discrimination

International Law:

(0) No recognition
(1) International law informs domestic law/source of law
(2) International law has constitutional or supra-constitutional status

Political Rights and Provisions

Equal Citizenship

(-1) Citizenship is passed only through the father
(0) No gender-specific statement or neutral language ("all persons")
(1) Gender equality is explicit; citizenship is passed by either mother or father

Equal Suffrage

(0) Neutral/no gender-specific statement about voting rights
(1) Gender-specific statement (sex cannot be a basis for denying the right to vote or women and men have an equal right to vote)

Equal Political Participation

(0) Neutral/no gender-specific statement about women's political participation
(1) Statement or principle about equal access to public office, rules about forming political parties, statement about women's equality in political life, or state encouragement of women's political participation
(2) State obligation or right to access and/or multiple statements about equal political participation of women

Quotas

(0) None specified at the constitutional level

(1) Mandate a minimum amount of female representation in elected or appointed bodies (national or sub-national level)
(2) Provision details gender quota size and enforcement

Government Commission

(0) No gender-based government body recognized
(1) Specified constitutional body: commission, ministry, or other oversight body
(2) Multiple gender-based bodies

Royal Descent

(−1) Male only
(0) Unspecified or gender-neutral
(1) Specifies men and women can inherit/be monarch

Social Rights and Provisions

Equality in Marriage and Family Law

(0) No statement about marriage, spousal, or family equality
(1) Statement about marriage, spousal, or family equality
(2) Gender-specific statement(s) about marriage, spousal, or family equality

Reproductive Health

(0) No statement
(0) Gender-neutral statement or general recognition of a right to health care
(1) Statement about reproductive health care (family planning, child spacing)
(2) Right to reproductive health services or state obligation to ensure access to reproductive health care

Gender-Based Violence

(0) No statement/rights
(0) Gender-neutral statement (e.g., bodily integrity, freedom from violence)
(1) Gender-specific statement about bodily integrity or freedom from violence
(2) State obligation to protect or ensure rights

Equality in Education

(0) No statement about access or right to education

(0) Gender-neutral statement about access or right to education
(1) Gender-specific statement about access or right to education
(2) State obligation to ensure equal access

Customary Law

(−2) Customary law exempt from constitutional rights
(−1) Ambiguous relationship
(0) No statement/no recognition
(1) Customary law is subordinate to constitutional rights

Family Protection

(0) No mention of family
(1) Family recognized as an important social unit
(2) State obligation to protect families and provide family allowances or multiple statements

Social Policy

(0) No mention of social rights or services
(0) Gender-neutral statement or recognition of social rights
(1) Statement about social policies based on gender, pregnancy, and motherhood
(2) State obligation to enact social policies based on gender, pregnancy, and motherhood

Abortion

(−2) Explicit ban on abortion
(−1) Right to life from conception (or the unborn or about to be born)
(0) No specific statement about abortion

Special Treatment (Other Than Social Policy, Family, or Labor Protection)

(0) No other special treatment on basis of gender, pregnancy, and marital status
(1) Women recognized in the same category as minors and/or mentally and physically disabled persons
(2) State obligation to treat women differently or multiple statements

Official Religion

(−1) Explicit constitutional recognition
(0) No statement or recognition

Economic Rights and Provisions

Equal Opportunity in the Workplace

(0) No equal opportunity language
(0) Gender-neutral statement about equal opportunity in public or private employment
(1) Gender-specific statement about equal access or opportunity in the workplace
(2) State obligation/positive actions to ensure equal opportunity

Equal Pay for Equal Work

(0) No equal pay for equal work statement
(0) Gender-neutral recognition (no mention of sex or gender)
(1) Gender-specific recognition of equal pay

Family Leave

(0) No leave
(1) Paternal or family leave recognized

Maternity Leave

(0) No leave
(1) Maternity leave recognized

Workplace Protection

(0) No mention of the rights of workers or workplace protection
(0) Gender-neutral recognition of labor protection or worker rights
(1) Gender-specific statement about labor protection or restrictions based on gender, pregnancy, and motherhood
(2) State obligation to ensure labor protection based on gender, pregnancy, and motherhood

Construction of Egalitarian and Maternal Provisions Indexes

The egalitarian provision score and the maternal provision score are based on a subset of the aforementioned provisions. The egalitarian score is a combined score based on the provisions which guarantee women's right to equality, non-discrimination, equal suffrage, equal citizenship, political participation, equality in marriage, reproductive health, freedom from gender-based violence, equal pay, and workplace equality. The highest possible score is 16 (Ethiopia's Constitution is the only one that earns 16 points on this index). We limited the index to these ten provisions because they were the most relevant to women's equality in the four policy areas we focus on throughout the book. Among the few provisions we did not include, are those such as royal descent that would have enjoyed equal weight to a more relevant right such as equal pay for equal work and may have skewed the results.

The provisions included in the maternal score are family protection, social policy guarantees, special treatment, maternity leave, and workplace protection. This index is also a combined score; the highest possible score is 9. The highest maternal score among our countries is Ecuador's Constitution in 2005 (8 points).

The range of egalitarian and maternal scores is summarized in Figures 2.1 and 2.2, respectively, in Chapter 2. The statistical analyses presented in Chapter 3 utilize the egalitarian and maternal scores for all countries with available data for the dependent and control variables. The countries and scores appear in Appendix B.

Notes

1 Constitutions of the Countries of the World is a project of Oxford University Press.
2 Elkins, Zachary, Tom Ginsburg, James Melton. Constitute: The World's Constitutions to Read, Search, and Compare. Online at constituteproject.org.
3 The Global Gender Equality Constitutional Database is available at: https://constitutions.unwomen.org/en.

APPENDIX B

Egalitarian and Maternal Constitutional Provision Scores, 1995–2015

Country	*Egalitarian 1995*	*Maternal 1995*	*Egalitarian 2005*	*Maternal 2005*	*Egalitarian 2015*	*Maternal 2015*
Afghanistan	.	.	1	2	1	2
Albania	0	0	1	4	1	4
Algeria	1	2	1	2	2	2
Andorra	2	2	2	2	2	2
Angola	.	.	.	.	5	5
Antigua & Barbuda	2	0	2	0	2	0
Argentina	4	3	4	3	4	3
Armenia	.	.	2	4	2	4
Australia	0	0	0	0	0	0
Austria	2	0	4	0	5	0
Bahamas	.	.	0	0	0	0
Bahrain	.	.	3	2	3	2
Bangladesh	5	0	5	0	5	0
Belgium	0	0	3	0	3	2
Benin	2	3	2	3	2	3
Bhutan	.	.	.	.	3	1
Bolivia	2	4	4	4	15	5
Bosnia & Herzegovina	.	.	.	.	1	0
Botswana	1	0	1	0	2	0
Brazil	8	6	8	6	8	6
Bulgaria	4	5	4	5	4	5

(Continued)

APPENDIX B (Continued)

Country	*Egalitarian 1995*	*Maternal 1995*	*Egalitarian 2005*	*Maternal 2005*	*Egalitarian 2015*	*Maternal 2015*
Burkina Faso	.	.	4	2	4	2
Cambodia	.	.	10	4	10	4
Cameroon	1	3	1	3	1	3
Canada	3	0	3	0	3	0
Cape Verde	5	5	5	5	5	5
Chad	.	.	3	2	3	2
Chile	0	2	2	2	2	2
China	.	.	7	3	7	3
Colombia	.	.	.	.	6	5
Comoros	.	.	.	.	2	0
Costa Rica	2	7	2	7	2	7
Croatia	.	.	1	5	1	5
Cuba	.	.	8	4	8	4
Czech Republic	0	0	1	4	1	4
Denmark	0	0	0	0	0	0
Dominica	2	1	2	1	2	1
Dominican Republic	3	3	3	3	12	5
Ecuador	.	.	13	8	14	7
Egypt	0	3	0	3	0	0
El Salvador	5	5	5	5	5	5
Estonia	3	2	3	2	3	2
Ethiopia	16	3	16	3	16	3
Fiji	.	.	.	.	2	0
Finland	4	2	4	2	4	2
France	1	0	2	0	3	0

Gambia	7	0	7	0	7	0
Georgia	.	.	2	3	2	3
Germany	3	2	3	2	3	2
Ghana	4	2	7	2	7	2
Greece	2	3	4	3	4	3
Grenada	3	0	3	0	3	0
Guatemala	4	7	4	7	4	7
Guinea	.	.	.	.	3	2
Guyana	5	3	5	3	8	0
Haiti	.	.	.	.	8	2
Honduras	3	7	3	7	3	7
Hungary	2	5	2	5	2	4
Iceland	1	0	1	0	1	0
India	7	3	7	3	7	3
Indonesia	0	0	0	1	0	1
Iran	1	6	1	6	1	6
Iraq	.	.	5	4	5	4
Ireland	1	5	1	5	1	5
Israel	.	.	0	0	0	0
Italy	5	4	7	4	7	4
Jamaica	.	.	2	0	2	0
Japan	4	0	4	0	4	0
Jordan	0	1	0	1	0	3
Kazakhstan	1	2	1	2	1	2
Kenya	.	.	2	0	9	1
Kiribati	0	0	0	0	0	0
Korea, Republic of	3	2	3	2	3	2
Kosovo	.	.	.	.	7	2

(Continued)

APPENDIX B (Continued)

Country	*Egalitarian 1995*	*Maternal 1995*	*Egalitarian 2005*	*Maternal 2005*	*Egalitarian 2015*	*Maternal 2015*
Kuwait	0	2	0	2	0	2
Kyrgyzstan	.	.	.	.	4	2
Latvia	.	.	0	2	0	2
Lebanon	.	.	0	0	0	0
Lesotho	3	1	3	1	3	1
Liberia	4	0	4	0	4	0
Liechtenstein	.	.	1	2	1	2
Lithuania	3	4	3	4	3	4
Luxembourg	.	.	1	1	3	1
Macedonia	.	.	3	3	3	3
Madagascar	.	.	4	4	5	4
Malawi	11	5	11	5	11	5
Malaysia	-1	0	-1	0	0	0
Maldives	.	.	.	.	2	1
Malta	.	.	4	0	4	0
Marshall Islands	1	0	1	0	1	0
Mauritania	2	2	2	2	3	2
Mauritius	.	.	1	0	1	0
Mexico	4	5	5	5	7	5
Micronesia	1	0	1	0	1	0
Moldova	2	5	2	5	2	5
Monaco	.	.	1	1	1	1
Mongolia	4	3	4	3	4	3
Montenegro	.	.	.	.	4	5

Morocco	1	0	1	0	4	3
Mozambique	.	.	.	.	5	2
Myanmar	.	.	.	.	2	3
Namibia	8	3	8	3	8	3
Nauru	0	0	0	0	0	0
Nepal	2	2	2	2	13	3
Netherlands	1	0	1	0	1	0
New Zealand	2	0	2	0	2	0
Nicaragua	10	6	10	6	10	6
Niger	.	.	.	.	8	3
Nigeria	.	.	3	0	3	0
Norway	1	0	1	0	1	0
Pakistan	2	4	2	4	2	4
Palau	3	0	3	0	3	0
Panama	6	7	7	7	7	7
Papua New Guinea	5	1	5	1	5	1
Paraguay	11	5	11	5	11	5
Peru	3	4	3	4	3	4
Philippines	2	5	2	5	2	5
Poland	.	.	5	6	5	6
Portugal	8	4	9	4	9	4
Romania	2	5	4	5	4	5
Russian Federation	1	5	1	5	1	5
Rwanda	.	.	.	.	5	2
Saint Lucia	2	0	2	0	2	0
Saint Vincent & Grenadines	2	0	2	0	2	0
Samoa	.	.	.	.	3	1
Sao Tome & Principe	5	2	5	2	6	2

(*Continued*)

APPENDIX B (Continued)

Country	*Egalitarian 1995*	*Maternal 1995*	*Egalitarian 2005*	*Maternal 2005*	*Egalitarian 2015*	*Maternal 2015*
Saudi Arabia	.	.	.	.	0	2
Senegal	.	.	.	.	9	3
Seychelles	.	.	.	.	1	2
Sierra Leone	.	.	.	.	3	2
Singapore	-1	0	-1	0	-1	0
Slovakia	.	.	2	5	2	5
Slovenia	4	2	6	2	6	2
Solomon Islands	.	.	.	.	2	0
Somalia	.	.	.	.	7	6
South Africa	8	0	8	0	8	0
South Sudan	.	.	.	.	7	6
Spain	4	2	4	2	4	2
Sri Lanka	4	3	4	3	4	3
Sudan	.	.	11	4	11	4
Surinam	5	5	5	5	5	5
Sweden	2	1	2	1	2	1
Switzerland	.	.	6	5	6	5
Taiwan	.	.	4	2	4	2
Tanzania	.	.	2	0	2	0
Thailand	.	.	4	3	6	3
Timor-Leste	.	.	6	4	6	4
Togo	.	.	.	.	5	2
Tonga	0	0	0	0	0	0
Trinidad and Tobago	1	0	1	0	1	0
Tunisia	.	.	.	.	7	2
Turkey	.	.	4	3	6	4

Tuvalu	1	1	1	1	1	1
Uganda	8	6	8	6	8	6
Ukraine	6	5	6	5	6	5
United Kingdom	1	0	2	0	2	0
United States	1	0	1	0	1	0
Uruguay	1	4	1	4	1	4
Vanuatu	2	0	2	0	2	0
Venezuela	.	.	7	5	7	5
Vietnam	.	.	.	.	7	3
Yemen	0	4	0	4	0	4
Zambia	3	0	3	0	3	0
Zimbabwe	.	.	.	.	11	5

INDEX

Note: Information in figures and tables is indicated by page numbers in *italics* and **bold,** respectively.

For Product Safety Concerns and Information please contact our EU representative GPSR@taylorandfrancis.com
Taylor & Francis Verlag GmbH, Kaufingerstraße 24, 80331 München, Germany

www.ingramcontent.com/pod-product-compliance
Ingram Content Group UK Ltd.
Pitfield, Milton Keynes, MK11 3LW, UK
UKHW022355190926
475702UK00015B/2304
* 9 7 8 1 0 3 2 3 0 1 6 1 7 *